RUSKIN COLLEGE

A Challenge to Adult and Labor Education

AL NASH

New York State School of
Industrial and Labor Relations
Cornell University

ISBN:087546-084-4

Copies of this book may be ordered from
ILR Publications
New York State School of Industrial
and Labor Relations
Cornell University
Ithaca, New York 14853

Library of Congress Cataloging in Publication Data

Nash, Al.
    Ruskin College, a challenge to adult and labor education

    Bibliography: p.
    1. Ruskin College.   2.   Adult education--England.
3.   Labor and laboring classes--Education--England.
I.   Title.
LF741.R83N37   374'.8'0942574   81-1231
ISBN 0-87546-084-4 (pbk.)   AACR2

Table of Contents

I.

Introduction

Ruskin College, a two-year school founded in Oxford in 1899, is the oldest residential labor college in the world. It is an independent, small college--seventy-six graduates in 1978--that in its first decade was subjected to a student strike that resulted in the founding of a rival school by dissatisfied students. Ruskin also has survived an attempted annexation by Oxford University, the financial problems caused by the depression, and the two world wars when operations were suspended. Throughout much of its existence, Ruskin has had to withstand criticism from the left and from the right. Despite these vicissitudes, Ruskin has received high grades for its academic standards. The school is highly respected by union leaders as well as by the academic community and by its own graduates.

Ruskin graduates have occupied high office in Parliament (eleven in 1978), local government, unions, universities, and adult education. R. H. Tawney and G. D. H. Cole are among the distinguished scholars who have served as consultants to its Governing Council as Lord Briggs and Lord McCarthy (a former Ruskin student) do now. Prime ministers, British educators, and foreign guests have visited Ruskin, and labor colleges have borrowed from its curricula and methods to enhance their own programs. Several well-known British writers (such as Max Beer) have noted that Ruskin graduates have contributed to the intellectual currents of their time as well as to the labor and socialist movements.[1]

The school has managed not only to survive but to grow, while other residential labor colleges in the United States and Great Britain have disappeared, yet little is known in the United States about Ruskin College. Those persons and organizations concerned with labor studies and continuing

1

education will find that a study of Ruskin will shed some light on the ongoing debates in Britain and the United States about curriculum, academic standards, and teaching methods as well as the nature of a labor college or its equivalent.[2] Moreover, the Ruskin experience is of special interest to those concerned about the relationship of class, status, a labor party, and a powerful union movement to a labor college and to workers whose educational opportunities have been limited. Finally, the Ruskin experience is a base from which to look at how the residential labor college, in contrast to the commuter college, affects the attitudes and aspirations of the students.

The major work on Ruskin is by Jay Blumler whose dissertation (Oxford University, 1962) is devoted to the effects of long-term residential education on adult students--mainly union members who attended Ruskin College. He found that the major effect of the long-term residential adult college is the increased confidence and poise acquired by the graduates. These qualities facilitate the ability of the graduate to climb the "social ladder." Blumler also noted that "although long-term residential study is often an agent of change, many of its effects either continue developments that had started before the college or reflect motives that had encouraged students to apply for admission." The school is able to play the role of "agent of change" because it has a social and political climate that is congruent with the values of the student and his or her motives for entering the school.[3]

Blumler drew his data from questionnaires completed by 180 Ruskin graduates who had entered the school between 1945 and 1953; from identical questionnaires completed, during the same period, by 199 graduates of four long-term residential adult colleges; a longitudinal study of 207 students who completed questionnaires upon entering and leaving Ruskin between 1952 and 1956; and from 79 Ruskin students interviewed prior to their graduation in 1956 and 1957.[4]

A study written by Harold Pollins, a senior tutor at Ruskin (as was Blumler), listed the major changes that began in 1968 in the government structure of the school as a result of pressure from Ruskin students and inspired in part by the revolt of Parisian students that year. From this study, he concluded that involvement of students in the government of the school is "time-consuming and repetitious, but these are an inevitable consequence of the recognition of student rights.[5]

Brief studies have been made by Ruskin students: A. W. M. Cattermole wrote a comparison of Ruskin with the Brunnsvik Folk High School of Sweden; Paul Yorke did a short history of Ruskin College from 1899 to 1909; and M. Smith focused on the social mobility of Ruskin graduates, using Blumler's questions or their equivalent with a more recent group of Ruskin graduates.[6] Much of the other literature on Ruskin was written in the first three decades of the twentieth century. It consists mainly of memoirs of Ruskin graduates or observations made by former tutors, who make passing references to the school or its graduates, and of studies of adult education as well as studies of the British labor movement. There are no current and detailed descriptions of the school in the literature, a gap I have attempted to fill with this study.

The data on which my report is based were collected from July through November of 1978 at Ruskin College where I had access to a twenty-thousand-volume library which included old documents, journals published by Ruskin students, copies of examinations, annual reports of the school, and articles about Ruskin. I also interviewed students, alumni, tutors, and the principal, H. D. Hughes. I became, in part, a participant-observer by lecturing occasionally, attending classes and other college events, and socializing with students and tutors. Notes were made of informal discussions, at conferences where Ruskin graduates spoke, and in classes where they taught.

Although the major aim of this investigation was a descriptive study of Ruskin and its students, it has also provided insight into the various influences and agencies that helped shape Ruskin College and its students. This report is a part of the results of my five months at Ruskin and of my study and experiences in labor education. In it I shall consider the background of Ruskin and its students, its social organization, its social and political climate, the impact of a residential college on labor students, and a comparison of Ruskin with other labor colleges. In the concluding section of the report I will deal more generally with conflict, ideology, and problems in a labor college, and, finally, with trends in Ruskin and other colleges.

II.

Historical Background of Ruskin

The shaping of Ruskin began with its founding in 1899 by the Americans Charles A. Beard and Walter Vrooman. Beard was then a socialist and graduate student at Oxford University and, later, a renowned historian. Vrooman was a Christian socialist and a philanthropist. He was also an admirer of John Ruskin, the art critic and forerunner of modern British socialism who denounced the evil effects of industrialization on the worker. The inscription on a photograph of Ruskin Hall sent by Vrooman, Beard, and other Ruskin faculty to John Ruskin expressed their feeling for the man for whom they named the college: "We build not alone in honor of Ruskin, the eloquent art critic, but to Ruskin the labourer, with his trouser ends turned up, with his pick and shovel on his shoulder, as he went to work to improve the roads about Oxford."[1]

The founders launched the college to offer working-class adults an opportunity to receive an education equivalent to that provided by Oxford University. Students were expected to acquire knowledge that would enable them to defend the interests of the working class not "by uttering tirades against society and institutions," but "by the use of scientific methods." The mission of the students and the high, if somewhat critical, opinion of Oxford held by the founders was grandiloquently summed up at the inauguration of Ruskin College by Vrooman when he said that "Ruskin students come to Oxford, not as mendicant pilgrims go to Jerusalem, to worship at her ancient shrines and marvel at her sacred relics, but as Paul went to Rome, to conquer in the battle of ideals."[2]

The ability to "conquer," however, depended on the emergence of conditions favorable to this objective. Beginning with the first decade of the twentieth century, economic and political conditions emerged that facilitated the expansion

of the labor movement and consequently of Ruskin. Changes
in the ideology, outlook, and goals of the labor movement
were to lead to restructuring some craft unions into general unions and to the formation of the Independent Labour
party (1899), the Socialist Labour party (1902), the Workers'
Educational Association (1903), and the Labour party (1906).[3]

It was during this period of unrest and change that
Ruskin was getting underway. The sudden growth and expansion of the organizations that made up the labor movement
created openings for full-time staff members that many
Ruskin graduates were able to fill. In turn, students were
attracted to Ruskin because it provided access to desirable
jobs in the labor movement and to knowledge useful in understanding and changing the social system. The needs of labor
organizations and worker-students coincided. Ruskin played
the role of middleman.[4]

Two-thirds of Ruskin students were and still are drawn
from Northern England, Wales, and Scotland--areas where the
workers are most class conscious. According to Anthony
Giddens, the miners and other isolated masses of British
workers, particularly those who live in Northern England,
Scotland, and Wales, are among the "archetypical" workers,
members "of a clearly distinct 'working-class culture,' and
strongly class conscious." Although there may have been
some changes in the degree of class consciousness and its
geographic distribution, British workers have remained among
the most class-conscious workers of the western democracies.
Richard Hoggart, for example, observed in 1957 that to be a
member of the British working class "is even now to belong
to an all pervading culture, one in some ways as formal and
stylised as any that is attributed to, say, the upper classes."
Raymond Williams later elaborated on the theme of "working-
class culture" and "bourgeois culture." He defined the former as "the basic collective idea, and the institutions,
manners, habits of thought and intentions which proceed from
this." The latter he described as "the basic individualist
idea and the institutions, manners, habits of thought and intentions which proceed from that."[5]

Examples of the "manners, habits of thought and intentions" are found in Seymour Lipset's comparison of American
and British values in which he emphasizes that the social
class system of the English "retains many elements of as-
cription, elitism, particularism, and diffuseness. The
traditional upper classes and their institutions--the public
schools, the ancient universities, and the titled aristocracy--

remain at the summit of the social structure." These
comments, which indicate the status gulf between the two
classes, are supported by the findings of the "Committee
of Inquiry..." into adult education appointed by the
Secretary of State for Education and Science and chaired
by Sir Lionel Russell (hereafter referred to as the Russell
Committee). In 1973, the committee reported that "educationally we are still Two Nations and among the educational 'have-nots' the needs are vast."[6]

The origin of Ruskin was in its own way a response to
the difference between the "Two Nations," as was a split
in 1909 between Ruskin and Plebs League--a group of students
who viewed the "academic" approach of the school as pro-
establishment. The difference between Ruskin and the Plebs
League also reflected the disagreements in and between working-class organizations such as the Labour party, the Socialist Labour party, the Social Democratic Federation, the Independent Labour party and the Workers' Educational Association
(WEA).* It was no accident that by 1908, when the Plebs League
was founded, the students of Ruskin were socialists of one
shade or another.[7]

It was in the context of these and the developments described earlier that Vrooman launched Ruskin College. One of
his reasons for establishing Ruskin was to educate workers
to influence and help workers as a class, which explains
why, from the beginning, the school sought the cooperation
of the labor movement. In its first years, Ruskin established
ninety-two correspondence classes in sixty-two cities and
towns and corresponded with almost eight thousand students
who were enrolled in the courses.[8] Through these efforts,
Ruskin attracted workers who were more influential in their
unions, more Marxist in outlook, and more sophisticated academically than the first students at Ruskin.

In view of the ideological orientation of students who
entered Ruskin, it was almost guaranteed that, as Brian Simon
noted, they would demand that teachers be less impartial and
less neutral in discussing social conflicts between workers
and capitalists. But, according to Raymond Challinor, "the

---

*Political sects often have as their main stock in trade
"education of the masses." From their point of view, this
may be "education" but from the point of view of others,
it is "propaganda." While Vrooman's socialist beliefs
were more Christian than Marxist, he, too, was a propagandist.

Ruskin establishment sought to destroy the socialist heresy. Greater emphasis was placed on the traditional approach to economics and sociology in the hope that it would finally gain acceptance. Then students would go back into the outside world as a stabilizing influence, perhaps taking trade union posts to counteract the influence of militancy." And, according to Geoff Brown, "highly placed and influential supporters of Ruskin and the WEA continually lauded the work of the two institutions for their potential as agencies of 'social control'."[9]

The argument that Ruskin was exerting "social control" on behalf of the establishment was based on the refusal of the school and most of its faculty to abandon the academic approach of maintaining detachment in discussing differences among working-class political parties and other segments of the labor movement, stimulating students to examine different points of view and to make use of empirical data. The students rejected this approach as unrealistic. They complained that the administration and faculty did not understand them as workers, were too rigid in trying to remedy educational weaknesses, and were intolerant of students who disagreed with them. Students and the Ruskin administration also disagreed about the relationship of Ruskin to Oxford University. The students felt that the administration was attempting to bring them under the social control of the university, the haven of the privileged classes.[10]

As a result of these differences and the social unrest that existed nationally, the Plebs League was organized by Ruskin students who were among the most class-conscious workers in a period that E. J. Hobsbawn called "the Golden Age of British Marxism and diffusion of Marxist ideas." Organization of the Plebs League was characterized by Raymond Postgate as the "first revolt" in the educational field by "worker-students"--students who "resented the capitalist economics taught at Ruskin College."[11]

Ruskin administration and faculty rejected the arguments of the Plebs League and claimed that it was clearly possible to combine scholarly aims with a strong sense of social purpose while pursuing a dispassionate search for the truth.*

---

*This approach still exists as may be noted in the comment of H. D. Hughes, Ruskin's principal from 1950 to 1979, who observed: "We do not give our students a pre-set idea, but rather we give them their independence of mind to operate effectively in their work" (interview, Oxford Mail, November 13, 1978).

The members of the league responded by petitioning the
Governing Council of Ruskin on which union leaders, including a representative of the Trades Union Congress
(TUC), served. The council rejected the petition unani-
mously and the dissident students seceded from Ruskin to
launch the Central Labour College (CLC). They had the
support of the miners, railway workers, and other segments of the labor movement. Six years later, in 1915,
after a persistent campaign by the CLC and its supporters,
the TUC officially recognized the school and cooperated
with it.[12] With the official endorsement of the TUC,
the CLC expanded by organizing more labor colleges that
joined to form the National Council of Labour Colleges
(NCLC) in 1921.

The departure of Pleb students and the resulting
rivalry between the two schools provoked Ruskin officials
into introducing a number of changes. Among the first
changes was a new constitution that gave representatives
of the labor movement a clear-cut majority on the Governing Council; other positions were set aside for members
of the academic community to serve in advisory roles. In
addition the curriculum was revised and, in general, members of the administration became more flexible.

The relationship between Oxford and Ruskin, no longer
burdened by the dissident students, soon improved as
"signalized in 1910 by the opening of the [Oxford] University Diploma in Economics and Political Science to
Ruskin candidates." By 1911, fourteen students had completed the requirements for this diploma and ten passed
with "distinction." All the students were "second-chance"
students who had left school at fourteen years of age or
younger.[13]

Additional changes were introduced as Ruskin grew
older. Increased financial support enabled the school to
open a new building in 1912 with more classrooms and residential facilities. In 1920 it was recognized as a school
of higher learning, and was awarded an annual grant by the
Ministry of Education. With this increase in funds, residential facilities for women were provided and the Oxbridge
tutorial system was introduced. During this period, the
school developed a relationship with the educationally influential WEA, which in turn became a source of able candidates who were interested in enrolling in Ruskin.*

---

*Since the first decade of the twentieth century, the WEA
has supplied a sizeable number of Ruskin's students. For

8

By 1968 however the students had begun to chafe at
what they considered a "paternal" atmosphere. They protested among other things the lack of student involvement
in the government of the school and in planning the curriculum, and the lack of a diploma in labor studies. As a
result, the Labour Studies Diploma was introduced and alternative ways of taking examinations for a diploma were
offered along with other changes. In 1973, again as a
result of student action, the school introduced a series
of changes that increased the number of diplomas offered,
liberalized the Oxford diploma (e.g., papers could be
written on Marxism), and provided broader student representation on the committees and councils of Ruskin.[14]
Since that time no other basic changes have been made by
the school.

In retrospect it appears that as a consequence of
the departure of members of the Plebs League, the school
increased its adaptability and, most of all, its independence. By refusing to accept the criticism of the Plebs
League and at the same time retaining its loyalty to the
TUC and its major supporters, Ruskin kept its close connections with the labor movement while preserving its
academic integrity. In short, compared to the CLC, Ruskin
was perceived by the labor movement and prospective students as an important source of future labor leaders and
staff members.

Although the CLC and its subsidiary, the NCLC, expanded their operations and the number of worker-students
they reached, the CLC had disappeared by 1929. By 1964
the NCLC, which had abandoned Marxism as its core program
and had adopted a viewpoint compatible with that of the
TUC, was absorbed by the TUC educational department as
part of a policy of rationalizing working-class education
in Great Britain. Ruskin, too, was affected by the new
policy and agreed to turn over its correspondence department to the TUC educational department. In exchange, more
unions utilized the college's services and supported it
financially and in other ways.

---

example, from 1926 to 1932, 64 percent of the 174 British
students who entered Ruskin were former WEA students in
adult education. See Geoff Brown, "Educational Values and
Working Class Residential Adult Education," p. 15.

Changes in the number of students at Ruskin have
taken place slowly. Beginning with 20 students in 1899,
the number of students increased to 54 just before the
"split" in the school ten years later. Although the correspondence section of the school remained active, the
residential section was closed during World War I, re-
opening in 1919. The total number of Ruskin graduates
from 1899 until the year it reopened was 500. During
the interval between the two world wars there were never
more than 35 enrolled in the school. During World War II,
Ruskin again suspended its residential program but continued its correspondence courses. Between 1945 and 1953,
as the school became more stable financially, an average
of 40 students were accepted yearly. By 1957, the number
of students rose to 138; between 1969 and 1978, the total
number registered each year averaged 170.[15]

III.

Ruskin's Administrative and Educational Setting

Ruskin, like other long-term residential colleges, operates on the assumption that attractive and functional facilities ease the adjustment of students away from home and make the enjoyment of the surroundings part of their education. At the same time, Ruskin recognizes, and was built on, academic principles that call for an organizational structure that defines academic procedures and standards and assures regularity and predictability in meeting the objective of a sound education for the adult-worker student.

FACILITIES AND COSTS

At present Ruskin College has two campuses. The Walton Street campus, where the main building stands, is near the center of Oxford. It is a grim squat affair shielding a modern residential building, several cottages, and a small garden behind it. The other, the Ruskin Hall campus, is located on the opposite side of Oxford (Headington), and consists of six small buildings at the end of a lane on twenty-two acres of land graced by groves of trees. The Walton Street campus houses the administrative staff, the majority of tutors, and most of the second-year resident students. Ruskin Hall houses a smaller number of tutors and first-year resident students. The school has residential facilities for 142 students. About 35 of the second-year students find other quarters in or near the city of Oxford. For the new students, Ruskin Hall is both attractive and functional. As for the main campus, Ruskin plans to expand those facilities in the near future.

11

One hundred twenty-nine persons are employed or paid a fee by Ruskin College: twenty-one are tutors, twenty-seven are part-time or ad hoc tutors, and three are officers; thirty-four are external examiners, including the Diploma Assessment Board; and forty-four are full- and part-time maintenance, culinary, and clerical workers.* This large staff is needed to support a residential college, and the high cost of such support may help explain why there are so few residential colleges for adults.

Where the individual Ruskin student is concerned, the cost in 1978 was about $2,000 at a minimum, including room, board, and tuition.[1] Six hundred dollars of this was for tuition. Because Ruskin is recognized by the Department of Education and Science (DES) as a residential school of higher learning and a "responsible body," its students are entitled to financial support from the local educational authorities and from the national government. The payments made to Ruskin and its students by local educational authorities and the DES are made possible by the Education Act of 1975. Salaries for tutors are also paid in part by the same sources. (The highest salary for a senior tutor in 1978 was about $12,000 a year.)

The minimum that an eligible, single student in the city of Oxford received in 1978 was about $2,030. In addition students could receive $960 a year for a spouse, or another dependent, and $370 for a dependent child. This support money could be supplemented by up to $500 in grants or scholarships that are awarded by unions, trusts, cooperatives, and other sources. In all, 207 scholarships and grants were paid for by the DES, TUC, its affiliates and other organizations in 1978. Students in financial distress can apply to the local social security office, local government authorities, and other agencies for supplementary rent allowance, food, and medical assistance.[2] Some students work between school terms to supplement their scholarships and grants (see Appendix A for particulars).

---

*A research group that provides the TUC and a number of its affiliates with economic data for collective bargaining purposes is also located at Ruskin. It is, however, financially and administratively independent of Ruskin College. Staff members of Ruskin, including the new principal, have cooperated with it and the work of the research group contributes to the scholarly reputation of the school.

In the academic year ending July 31, 1978, Ruskin
received more than $520,000 from the DES or 57 percent
of its total income of $921,490. It also received $104,176
or 11 percent of its income from the Department of Health
and Social Security. Twenty-five percent of its income
was from student fees, 5 percent from summer schools and
rents, and 1 percent from miscellaneous sources. Its total
expenditures for the same year were $905,836.[3]

THE COLLEGE ADMINISTRATION

The chief administrative officers are the principal,
vice-principal, and general secretary. The principal
during my visit was H. D. Hughes, who is now retired. He
was the chief administrative officer from 1950 to 1979.
During his term, he taught occasionally, served on school
committees, and met with the Governing Council. The relation of the principal to the council is similar to that of
the president of an American university to its trustees.
The vice-principal assists the principal in some of his
major responsibilities. J. D. Hughes, vice-principal during my stay at Ruskin, also teaches, writes, and plays an
important role as liaison to the Trade Union Research Unit
housed at Ruskin. He is a well-known economist and was
advisor in economic matters to the Labour party and the TUC.
The general secretary is responsible for most of the detailed
administrative matters including the introduction of new
students to the rules and procedures of Ruskin and to their
responsibilities as students.
Ruskin College's Governing Council consists of sixty-
six members. Sixty-one of them are representatives of
unions, including the TUC, and two are representatives of
the Workers' Educational Association (WEA). The D. H. Dains
Trust, the Ruskin Fellowship, and the Co-operative Union have
one representative each. Three prominent academic figures
hold consultative positions on the council. It meets once a
year and its executive committee, which is concerned with
major problems and decisions of the school, meets four times
a year.
In addition to the council, there are six diploma boards,
the Board of Studies, and the Academic Board. In addition,
there are other committees such as the General Purpose,
Teaching Aid, Library, and House Committees. Tutors and representatives of the Ruskin Students Union (RSU) jointly serve

13

on most of these boards and committees. According to a senior spokesperson that I interviewed (October 1, 1978),* Ruskin has "a very extensive program of joint discussion on practically every aspect of college life, including the Academic Board. A number of changes in course patterns, assessment methods, and so on have been introduced in response to student wishes." Asked whether these changes have made the school more sensitive or more formal, he responded:

> I think joint consultation had made it
> much more formal in the sense that things
> have to be put through joint committees
> and this leads to papers and documents
> and so on whereas before the joint com-
> mittees were introduced the process of
> decision making was more flexible and
> less formal.

Since 1968 the major differences between the RSU and the college "have been over College Administration and other procedural matters generally."[4] Some students believe that the rules pertaining to participation in decision making are not sufficiently broad. Most tutors believe that joint participation of students and tutors on committees is acceptable--even if burdensome.

EDUCATIONAL PROGRAMS

Students at Ruskin can choose between a two-year program built around one of the six types of diplomas (or majors) that are available or an individually tailored program. The individual program, however, does not lead to a diploma but to a Certificate of Studies which is less highly valued.**

---

*Where respondents have objected to the use of their names, I refer to them by pseudonyms or general titles. Citations from interviews are indicated by the date of the interview noted in parentheses.

**Students are permitted to work toward this Certificate of Studies or to attend Ruskin for one instead of two years. Few students choose either of these options; they prefer one of the six major diplomas. Unions and universities are more

The six types of diplomas are literature, history, social studies, development studies, applied social studies--which is accompanied by a Certificate of Qualification for Social Work, and labor studies. The two-year diploma programs consist of three ten-week terms each year.*

To qualify for the literature diploma, a student spends one term each on Shakespeare, poetry, drama, and the novel or an individual study topic. The student is also required to learn a foreign language and study the relationship between ideas, thought, life and literature, and the social classes of a specific period.

The history diploma, aimed at those planning to do research or to teach British history, requires that the student write on a specific topic of interest based on original study. The curriculum includes British history since 1760, nineteenth-century life and thought, the history of London, European history from 1830 to 1941, international affairs since 1918, and Irish history from 1800.

The social studies diploma requires a course of study in at least two social science disciplines leading either to an Oxford University Special Diploma in Social Studies or an equivalent Ruskin College diploma. The student can study economics, modern history, politics, or sociology. Whichever subjects are chosen, one must be studied on a theoretical level and the other on an applied level. If he or she prefers, the student may write a thesis on some related subject, for example British history after 1860, social and economic statistics, industrial relations, or Marxism.

The development studies diploma is intended for overseas students who are concerned about the formation, planning, and appraisal of economic and social development policies and who are involved, for example, with unions, cooperatives, or adult education. This course of study

---

likely to recognize the value of a diploma than a certificate or mere attendance at Ruskin. (Shorter courses of six weeks or less are also offered for officers of national unions, the TUC, and union stewards.)

*Most of the observations that follow are based on Ruskin College, Oxford Prospectus, 1978-1979.

deals with the special problems of former colonies ("low-income countries") and helps the student gain a broader understanding of the process of development. Development studies "is not a professional course of training in any aspect of development." The program is aimed primarily at those working in "development" organizations, unions, adult education, cooperatives, and community organizations. Because English is a second language for most of these students emphasis is placed on learning the basics of English. Emphasis is also placed on agricultural econ- omics, international economics, and the function of co- operatives.

The course leading to the Diploma in Applied Social Studies is substantially different from the other courses. It is vocationally oriented and is limited to fifteen stu- dents each year. Students in this program are referred to Ruskin by social service agencies that pay their salaries while they study. In exchange, each student agrees to re- main at the agency for two years after receiving the diploma. The minimum age of students in this program is twenty-five and, as a whole, they are older than students in other courses. The curriculum is built around the principles of social administration, sociology, psychology, and social work. The students are also introduced to practical field work. Applied social studies is the only program that has attracted more women than men; about 50 percent of the women students enroll in this course.

Many students consider labor studies the major program of the school and the most relevant for understanding the labor movement and contemporary social, political, and economic events. It was introduced to help union students who sought jobs in the labor movement rather than "academic honors" to enter universities. Requirements for the Labour Studies Diploma are typical of those of the other diplomas. It permits a number of choices to be made from the curriculum. The student may select four subjects, one of which may be his or her major, from at least three of the four areas offered or the student may select a pair of subjects from each of two areas. The four areas are: (1) Historical Development of Labour Movements, Development of Socialism, and Litera- ture and Society, (2) Social and Political Theory and In- stitutions, Labour Law, and Industrial Sociology, (3) In- dustrial Economics, and (4) the British Trade Union Move- ment, Comparative Industrial Relations, and Methods and

16

Sources of Labour Statistics.* Compulsory subjects in
this major are English Expression, Statistics, and
Industrial Relations. A thesis is required for the
Labour Studies Diploma. (See Appendix B for a more
complete description of the Diploma Course in Labour
Studies.)

The most popular major at Ruskin is social studies.
Of the 710 diplomas awarded between 1970 and 1979, 37
percent were in social studies, 28 percent in labor
studies, 17 percent in applied social studies (accompanied by the Certificate of Qualification for Social
Work), 8 percent in literature, 6 percent in development
studies, and 4 percent in history.[5] In part, the popu-
larity of the Diploma in Social Studies may be because
it facilitates entrance to Oxford or to other universities.**

A student at Ruskin must decide by the end of the
first term or, in some cases, by the end of the second
term, which diploma he or she intends to study for. A
student may decide not to study for any of the six
diplomas, an option that few exercise. This option,
however, provides an opportunity for a student to select
a combination of topics or subjects. If the subjects
are not available at Ruskin, the student is permitted to
turn to a friendly Oxford don or to a tutor at another
school in Oxford.

---

*The curricula offered by Ruskin in 1899 and 1978 are
similar in their liberal education approach. For instance,
the curriculum of 1899 included the Works of John Ruskin,
Writing English, English Grammar, English Constitutional
History, Political Economy, Sociology (fifty years before
it was offered at Oxford University), Speaking and Public
Work, and Industrial History. There were elective courses
such as French, Chaucer, Algebra, Metal Workers and Their
Guilds, and History of Christianity. The curriculum of
1899, however, offered little on unionism and related subjects.

**The desire of Ruskin students to go on to other schools
of higher education is influenced by the fact that universities have become more accessible and there is more financial assistance given to students by government agencies.
Also, as in the United States, more workers in Great Britain

On any matter related to a course, a student may appeal to a joint board of tutors and students that exists for each diploma course. If a change is desired that affects a diploma course, it must be approved by the Academic Board, which has an approximately equal number of tutors and students; the latter are selected by their peers.[6]

Compared to the conventional school and university, Ruskin permits far more participation by the student and the student union in the selection of courses and diplomas and in influencing the character of both. In this sense, it resembles a number of "innovating" colleges in the United States and the United Kingdom.

TEACHING METHODS

In keeping with the principle of student involvement in the educational process, the core of all teaching at Ruskin is the tutorial method, derived from the practice at Oxford and Cambridge. Each term a student selects a particular subject, is assigned to a subject tutor, and meets weekly with the tutor or with the tutor and another student studying the same subject. An advisory tutor is also available to the student.

Each student is free to select subjects for study, but within certain limits (and within the programs chosen) because it is considered undesirable to concentrate on a single subject to the exclusion of other social science disciplines. The educational approach at Ruskin is based on the belief that a genuine understanding of labor institutions and their problems requires a broad appreciation of relevant subjects in the humanities and the ability to work at a relatively advanced level within a specialty and by combining different specialties.

The weekly meeting with the subject tutor is built around an essay written by the student on some aspect of his or her major or on a topic assigned by the tutor. From four to eight 2,000-word essays are required each ten-week term, and some tutors encourage the student to submit an essay twenty-four hours in advance of the

---

and their children want the credentials that a university education can provide for obtaining better paying and more interesting jobs.

18

tutorial so the tutor can read it before the meeting.
At the tutorial, the student reads the essay aloud while
the tutor makes notes and raises questions. The tutor
also probes, spars, and answers each of the student's
questions with a question. Thus, the student is helped
to evaluate the evidence and to examine different approaches, discarding one possibility for another. In
discussing the tutorial system, Will G. Moore wrote:

> The whole process turns around the
> concept of bias: how you see things,
> how you evaluate evidence, how you
> tend to connect one fact with another.
> The student soon learns the teacher's
> mind, that a certain teacher tends to
> apply certain criteria or to favor cer-
> tain types of evidence. From this
> point onwards the good student will ac-
> quire independence of the teachers,
> will grope after his own means of
> interpretation.

The tutors help the students correct their own errors
and develop a cogent and logically ordered essay buttressed with the necessary evidence. Thus, they learn to
apply the criteria for critical judgments and take on
more responsibility for their own education. As Tim
Costello put it, "to write about a poem, a problem in
philosophy or a painting....is also to define the nature
of self. And if adult education is about anything it is
about enabling those who partake of it to achieve finer
and finer degrees of self-definition."[8] The tutor plays
a key role in the process by using a student's work as
the basis for discussion and by being sympathetic and
patient when criticizing it.

Among the chief qualities demanded of a tutor at
Ruskin as well as in workers' education (and in adult
education of which workers' education is a specialized
branch) are experience in teaching adults, particularly
union members, skill in presenting and understanding
other viewpoints, and the ability to make use of the
practical experience of the students, and, if at all
possible, experience as an active union member. In
addition the tutor must have a working knowledge of
several social sciences, mastery of a discipline,

patience, freedom from dogma, and a "good university degree."[9] Few tutors in workers' education possess all of these attributes, but in practical terms, a school like Ruskin seeks a tutor with a modest number of these qualities and particularly one who, according to H. D. Hughes (interview, October 1978), is "sympathetic to workers' education and workers." The school also prefers tutors who are former manual workers, but such persons are difficult to find as is reflected in the ability of Ruskin to recruit only two tutors who were manual workers.

Although tutors are not officially required to publish, most believe that they are expected to do so. As one tutor, Denis Haffner, explained in an interview (October 1978), "I think it is expected that we will produce something either in written form or perhaps from a teaching point of view. It is only that the expectation is not made explicitly as in the universities." This opinion does not seem to be shared by a spokesperson for the school. According to him, "tutors are given vague encouragement to write but they're not expected to do so. It's very much a teaching post and the teaching load is a fairly heavy one. We can't do more than give general encouragement to research...and writing activities." Whatever the expectation, most Ruskin tutors publish, either books or articles for journals or both. A tutor is expected to have a degree from a school of higher education. Of the twenty-one tutors at Ruskin in 1978, ten had a bachelor's, ten a master's, and one a doctorate.*

Although Ruskin places its main emphasis on tutorial methods, tutors are also expected to lecture. The tutors I observed were competent in their respective disciplines although conventional in their classroom procedure. Most of the students did not take notes, and those who did took them sparingly. In some classes, the relationship between the tutors and the students was stiff, perhaps because I was observing them at the beginning of a new academic year before an informal relationship had an opportunity to develop. In the classes

---

*A bachelor's degree in Great Britain may be somewhat higher in status and educational importance than a bachelor's degree in the United States.

where the students appeared to be in agreement with the tutor's philosophy relations were more informal and the majority of students raised questions or commented on the tutor's remarks.

The content of most lectures I heard indicated that most of the tutors had relatively high expectations in the academic work they demanded of the students. An example of the work expected by some tutors may be noted in the reading assignments for the course entitled "Management of the National Economy." The readings for an eight-week period included two textbooks and one to four chapters from twenty-six other books by authors such as John Maynard Keynes, Joan Robinson, and H. A. Clegg.

Attendance at classroom lectures is voluntary, poor, and was often deprecated by students and tutors with whom I spoke. Both agreed that the classroom lectures do not encourage student self-reliance or add to the tutor's ability to assess each student's rate of development or particular problems. One prominent Ruskin official pointed out that "the students could perfectly well go through Ruskin and do exceedingly well with never entering a class." Nevertheless, there is a greater emphasis on lectures for the first-year students in order to facilitate the transition from the classroom-teaching methods with which they are familiar to the tutorial method with which they have had little experience. Classroom teaching is also useful for first-year students because it makes peer support possible for those students who experience strain on returning to school. Written materials also help the new students know what to expect. For each major there was a detailed statement indicating what subjects the student would study in the next two years in order to earn a diploma.

In addition to tutorials and lectures, other forms of education are used at Ruskin. These include seminars, classes at Oxford University dons, lectures by nationally known scholars and figures, and the use of the Ruskin library and Oxford University's libraries.

STUDENT ASSESSMENT

Ruskin tutors are responsible for reports on each of their students. These reports are a part of the assessment system. Before a student's report is referred

to the principal at the end of each term, the student
is given a copy so that he or she can react to the
tutor's assessment of the term's work. The report
deals with the student's breadth of reading, depth of
understanding, analytical skills, quality of written
and oral expression, originality, critical judgment,
and independence of mind. Special attention is given
by the principal to the term reports of students ex-
periencing academic difficulties. (See Appendix C.)

Another form of student assessment at Ruskin is
through a thesis requirement. Each candidate for a
Labour Studies Diploma or a Diploma in Development
Studies is required to submit a thesis of about fifteen
thousand words.* The thesis is assessed by an internal
tutor and by a tutor from another school, often from
Oxford. The thesis done with tutorial supervision
enables a student to discover what level of work he
or she can achieve beyond the relatively restricted
range of normal tutorial assignments. Preparing the
thesis also allows genuine originality of work and
provides valuable training in thought and study through
the use of original materials.

Other types of assessment are used to determine
how well a student has done in a particular course.
A student may elect to write a paper within forty-
eight hours after receiving a topic.** Another

---

*Examples of student theses are: "The West Indian Fed-
eration: Why It Failed," "An Alternative Theory of Knowledge," "Popularism--The Revolt Against the Poor," "Labour
Studies of Women," "British Communism, Which Road?" and
"Studies in Alienation." My impression was that these
and other student theses that I read were better written and more scholarly than essays by undergraduates in
labor or industrial relations colleges in the United
States.

**For example, a student taking a forty-eight-hour exam
in Labour Movement History is required to answer four
questions and is given a choice from twelve questions
divided into two categories. Two examples from each
category are: (A) "Examine the principles of 'mutual
insurance' in the development of trade unions between
1815 and 1889," and "Account for the spread of industrial conciliation in the 1860's and 1870's." (B) "What

alternative is an hour written examination, which may be
an open-book exam. Most examination questions are
phrased in the form of a dilemma or a debatable statement.*

In summarizing the standards and methods of assessment, a Ruskin student wrote:

> Academic standards are rigorously main-
> tained by insisting [that] historians,
> say, acquire a reading knowledge of French,
> or social scientists, a mastery of statis-
> tics, and, above all, by [the use of] mod-
> erators, examiners, lecturers, subject ad-
> visors from the universities. Moreover,
> performance is graded for all Diplomas--
> Pass, Credit, Distinction--as are termly
> tutor reports.[10]

Since this summary was written, Ruskin has substituted
letter grades for the pass/credit/distinction system.
Grades run from A to C with C being designated as
"below standard."

The major complaints of Ruskin students are about
examinations and other methods of evaluating their
work. In an informal discussion, the students said,
in effect, that examinations stimulate competition,
are imitative of bourgeois values, and alienate the
student from education. According to the Agenda
(1978), a publication of the RSU, students would prefer to replace exams with "continuous assessment of
student, options of examination or continuous assessment for diplomas in all boards."

---

lessons did labour learn from their interwar period of
office?" and "In what way did the First World War
strengthen the institutions of the labour movement?"

*One three-hour exam in "Politics" contained twelve
questions from which the student was to choose four,
examples of which follow: (1) "Britain does not like
'coalition government.' Discuss." (2) "Parliamentary
Socialism: is there a contradiction in terms?"   (3)
"The effectiveness of a trade union as a pressure group
depends very little on the sponsorship of M.P.'s."
(4) "Discuss 'open government.' What are the necessary limitations?"

IV.

The Ruskin Students

Of the handful of British long-term residential colleges, Ruskin is the only one that gives preference to recruiting early school leavers who have been active in unions, in the Workers' Educational Association, or in a working-class community. Ruskin is also one of a small number of schools in higher education that use the tutorial method. Despite the demands made on the students who have not attended school for ten or more years, few drop out--perhaps one or two a year. Ruskin's recruitment criteria, its selection process, who the candidates are, and their motivation account for why they adapt so well to its stringent requirements.

RECRUITMENT AND SELECTION

The recruitment of applicants for Ruskin begins well in advance of the autumn semester. Each November, Ruskin mails a prospectus to unions, cooperatives, WEA branches, and other organizations that relate to the labor movement. A prospective student has until the following March to submit an application. (See Appendix D for a copy of the application form.) This involves filling in a detailed questionnaire and writing an essay on a topic in, for example, economics, politics, history, or social problems. According to H. D. Hughes (interview, August 1978), "By the time of the deadline, there will be, probably, between four hundred and five hundred applicants for the one hundred or so openings for first-year students."

Criteria for evaluating the applicants for admission are (1) activity in unions, cooperatives, and other labor organizations; (2) service to the community; (3) evidence of the ability to cope with Ruskin courses and the demands made upon a student by a residential college; and (4) an age between twenty and forty years. Preference is given to the educationally underprivileged or early school leaver. In addition, an applicant must demonstrate an awareness of the social as well as the personal benefits of further education. The school also attempts to keep a balance between the recruitment of manual and nonmanual workers.

Ordinarily every prospective student is interviewed by a committee consisting of the principal, two tutors, and two students. When a union member applies for a scholarship offered by his or her union, the general secretary of the union or its educational officer may be present at the interview. Each party--school or union--has a right to a veto. The school, however, may offer another type of scholarship if the union vetoes an applicant the school deems worthy of admission. The average interview takes about thirty minutes. At the end of the process, the committee makes its decision about who is to be admitted. The procedure in a typical interview was described by Haffner (October 1978):

> Before the prospective student comes in,
> we have his essay which we have looked
> at. Say it's on incomes policy. We
> have got his paper record which tells us
> about his background, his school, his
> job, his role in the trade union move-
> ment, why he wants to come, etc. So the
> thing is to probe his record, probe his
> motivation, and probe his ability. We
> do this by picking a topic from his essay
> or possibly picking up some other topic
> that he shows interest in and then ex-
> plore it with him in depth to see how
> far he can analyze and think.

H. D. Hughes believes that a worker who applies for admission to Ruskin must already be motivated to consider giving up a job and income for the chance and uncertain future of a latecomer to education. "It means, he said, "that we do attract rather exceptional people who, given the breaks, then emerge as cabinet ministers, university lecturers, trade union leaders, etc." (interview, August 1978). The recruitment committee, according to the tutors I interviewed, takes its duties seriously and rejects

25

applicants who would be unable to cope with the strains and tensions of returning to school as adults and as "second-chance" students.

STUDENT BACKGROUNDS: POLITICAL AND OCCUPATIONAL

Many successful applicants have already overcome some of their educational handicaps through such adult education programs as the WEA. According to Blumler, participation in these programs may have contributed to their desire to enter Ruskin while also preparing them academically to meet its standards. In addition, a majority of Ruskin students were and continue to be recruited from among exceptionally active members of unions, working-class parties, and cooperative societies. Blumler found that four-fifths of the employed Ruskin entrants were from local unions and adult education organizations. "Only 7 percent of the entrants were not members of labor organizations" in 1957. He also noted that 94 percent of Ruskin students during that period were members of the Labour party, 3 percent of the Communist party, and 3 percent distributed among the Conservative, Cooperative, and Liberal parties.[1] In 1978 Labour party membership declined to 63 percent and the percentage of students who were members of the Communist party, Socialist Workers party, and other radical sects appeared to have increased. Unfortunately, I do not have specific data for the minor political organizations.

When Ruskin tutors and alumni were asked what contributed to the ability of former students to acquire high-status jobs, one of the answers often given was "the old boys' network," although little evidence was offered to support this claim. The discussion, however, brought out that the example of graduates obtaining prestigious jobs plays a role in persuading others to enter Ruskin in the hope that they will be able to emulate their predecessors. In turn, the example of many union members seeking to enter Ruskin and the number of graduates who find high-status jobs prompt leaders of unions--especially new unions--and of other labor organizations to recruit Ruskin students for staff jobs.

Unions have been meticulous about whom they refer to Ruskin. They select members they think will make use of the education for the welfare of the labor movement.[2] Since the beginning of the first decade of the twentieth century, as I have suggested earlier, students referred to Ruskin by their unions were described by Lord Sanderson, a former Ruskin tutor, as "socialists of one brand or another, and there were amongst them some of the wildest and most revolutionary young men in the country." Students were drawn mainly from the ranks of skilled workers and Lord Sanderson described the great majority of them as "strongly imbued with socialism, varying from the mildest type to the most revolutionary form."[3] In 1899 virtually all of the students were members of unions. By 1978 the percentage of union members in Ruskin had declined to 67. There was also a shift from manual to nonmanual workers.[4] Finally, there was an increase in the number and percentage of students who were stewards at the time of entry into Ruskin.[5]

Of the twenty students who were enrolled in Ruskin in 1902-1903, seventeen were skilled workers, two were union officials, and one was a clerical worker. By 1958, 34 percent of the students had been clerical workers. By 1969 students who had been clerical or nonmanual workers made up 37 percent of the student body, skilled workers 23 percent, unskilled and semiskilled manual workers 21 percent, professionals 7 percent, and "other" 12 percent.[6] Interviews with Ruskin tutors and the principal (autumn 1978) disclosed that in the years 1976-78 approximately 75 percent of the students were either skilled or nonmanual workers before entering Ruskin.

Of the first-year students--those who entered in 1977--52 percent were former manual workers and 48 percent were nonmanual workers. (Seven students were not counted because they were listed as unemployed or occupation unknown.) Skilled and non-manual workers composed 81 percent of the students who entered the following year as first-year students.[7]

Tutors generally agreed that former skilled and nonmanual workers are more qualified to fill the student role than unskilled and semiskilled workers.[8] A spokesman (interview, September 1978) noted that the skilled worker "will at least have been through an apprentice course. He will, therefore, have some

27

kind of preparation which the unskilled workers would not have."

MOTIVATION AND AIMS OF THE STUDENTS

In part because of their union experiences and working-class backgrounds, Ruskin students tend to be more motivated to meet their academic responsibilities than the typical young undergraduates who attend college because it is expected of them or urged upon them by parents. Tutors perceive their mature students as "more eager to learn," more desirous of doing their best at everything they do, and according to Haffner (interview, October 1978), more likely to see the connection between what they learn and their roles on the job, in the community, and in the union. Ruskin students do not need teachers to try constantly to motivate them. They are more stimulating and stimulated. The Ruskin student, like the adult-education student, tends to be oriented to the present and to seek immediate practical solutions to problems.

In part, this eagerness to learn may relate to the desire to get a better job, to grow intellectually, and to reform or change the social order. Some observers of contemporary Ruskin students agree that their dominating drive is to get a better job. On the other hand, Geoff Brown notes that the students of the early 1900s, in keeping with the wishes of the founders of Ruskin and the pressures of their shopmates, returned to their former jobs and to their communities to assist in changing society. But by the 1930s this was no longer true. In an analysis of 500 Ruskin and WEA students in 1936, W. E. Williams and A. E. Heath observed that "of those who go to residential colleges the large majority are seeking to transfer themselves from the bench or the pit-face or the desk to organizing or teaching jobs in the working-class community." Smith and others have noted that Ruskin graduates still prefer jobs in a union and, if no jobs are available there, in organizing for the Labour party, teaching in adult or labor education, or working in local government.[9]

Smith compared the choice of employment of 1966-68 Ruskin entrants with the actual jobs they held in 1974 and discovered that although 33 percent opted for union

jobs at the time of entry, six years later only 8
percent held union jobs. Only 21 percent of the
1966-68 entrants wanted jobs in teaching, lecturing,
or research; by 1974, however, 44 percent were
employed in academic work. Whether jobs in unions
were not available or the entrants' aspirations
changed as a result of their experiences at Ruskin is
not clear.[10]

Many writers and observers agree that students
are motivated to attend Ruskin for intellectual and
cultural reasons. According to Blumler, nine-tenths
of his respondents came to Ruskin because they felt
intellectually inadequate and "inferior." They strongly desire to overcome these handicaps by acquiring "a
broader outlook and the equipment of a more logical
mind."[11] Some students, according to a Ruskin tutor,
David Selfridge (interview, October 1978), may have
entered Ruskin to support their political beliefs.
Other observers, especially Ruskin tutors, believe
students enter Ruskin for vocational purposes. My
analysis of reasons given by fifty-five new students
for registering at Ruskin showed that 42 percent
said "to further my education;" 33 percent, "to obtain
more knowledge about unions;" 10 percent, "to secure a
union job;" and 4 percent, "to go full time." Three
percent fell into a miscellaneous category and 8 percent did not list their reasons.

Between 1899 and 1909 many Ruskin students,
according to Yorke, may have enrolled to bask in the
reflected glory of Oxford, some came from abroad to
learn English, and "a few came out of a sense of
Christian duty." Finally, R. D. Sealey, a former
Ruskin student, noted that there are two categories
of students who have attended Ruskin:

> The first is those who have precon-
> ceived ideas of what they will be and
> where they are going, who are using
> Ruskin as a stepping stone for their
> preconceived objectives. Initially
> they maintain that they will change
> in no way. They are going back to
> the factory floor to carry on the
> fight. Not for them the university....
> Yet they change....The other group
> does not know where they are going
> or what they want.[12]

29

Presumably, those who change go on to a university, the other group is lost, without a sense "of purpose," and may eventually drop out of the school and return or drift back to the shop.

A more realistic approach to understanding the motives and aims of Ruskin students is to view them as "mixed." The workers become students because they wish (1) to "serve" the labor movement, (2) to obtain a full-time job in the labor movement, (3) to learn "precise and analytical habits," or (4) to strengthen their self-confidence.[13] Whatever their opinion of the students' aims, most tutors and graduates agree that students are deeply motivated and committed to getting the best out of their two-year stay at Ruskin. They also agree that recruiting candidates who are activists leads to enrolling students who are prone to become dissidents.

Pollins, for example, wrote: "It would be naive of course to ignore the fact that our preference for activists, which inevitably produces some students of the differing political sects, leads to conflicts of opinion within the study body. The RSU meetings, presumably, become a battleground between different factions." And from interviews with tutors (autumn 1978):

> Ruskin attracts the oddball who hasn't got a slot to fit into and seeks Ruskin as that slot. He's looking around for something to do different to what he has been doing. And they perhaps see Ruskin as the kind of institution which can offer them a complete change.

> If a college of this kind didn't attract people who have strongly held views that they were going to try and argue about very seriously and vigorously, it wouldn't be doing its job. We have to attract people like that--so it's part of the process and on the whole it's done more good than harm.

As these quotations indicate, activists may also be dissenters, and, in part, they are motivated to enter Ruskin to become more effective dissenters.

DEMOGRAPHIC PROFILE

Perhaps one reason many Ruskin students have been contentious and polemical has been their relative youth. For example, the average age of the students of the class of 1976-78 was 31.3 years, young enough to be optimistic about their ability to effect changes in society and to strive for a second chance to shape occupational, intellectual, and other major aspects of their lives. As a matter of fact, Ruskin seldom accepts students over forty years of age. The women students at Ruskin have generally been older than the male students.

Between 1945 and 1953, 16 percent of the Ruskin students were women; during the period from 1970 to 1978, 17 percent were women.[15] The absence of a significant increase in women students was commented on by a senior school official (interview, October 1978):

> We say we are equally open to men and
> women and we are. We only get 10 percent
> of women applicants largely because of
> our age group, which is in practice 20
> plus to 40 plus which is the period in
> which married women would find it diffi-
> cult to get away from their family respon-
> sibilities so that we have about 10 per-
> cent women overall in the college. The
> social work group recruits about 50 per-
> cent....We are under constant pressure
> from the students to try to recruit more
> women and we would be delighted to do so
> if they presented themselves, but we
> have not gone in for positive discrimi-
> nation. In other words, women are
> expected to meet the same criteria as
> men applicants. I suppose other things
> being equal, if it was a marginal candi-
> date we would say, "Ah, well, she's a
> woman, give her a place."

Ruskin is even less successful in recruiting blacks and Asians who are British citizens or immigrants and who have lived in Britain for three years or more (the time necessary to be eligible for a DES scholarship) than in recruiting women.[16] Asked to comment on this, principal Hughes said (interview, September 1978):

31

> We are equally open to blacks and whites.
> We have one or two scholarships designed
> for immigrants and our overseas program
> is heavily biased in the direction of
> students from East Africa, West Africa,
> and the West Indies....We finish up
> with 10 to 15 percent membership in the
> college of black students, either immi-
> grants to this country or coming direct
> from the developing world.

Mainly overseas blacks rather than black immigrants or
black British citizens are recruited as students. For
instance, in the 1977-78 academic year, there were fifteen overseas students, mainly from third-world countries.
Overseas recruitment by Ruskin goes back to 1902 but in
that era it was overseas Europeans who were recruited.

Overseas blacks are enrolled primarily in courses
leading to a development studies diploma. There is no
outreach program for British blacks and Asians since
Ruskin does not actively solicit students from any group.

Information on marital status was available for only
116 students in 1978. Ruskin's records showed that of
these 43 percent were married with children, 7 percent
were married and childless, 38 percent were single, 7
percent were separated, 4 percent were divorced, and 1
percent were widowed. In all, 50 percent were married,
which suggests that Ruskin students have more responsibilities than conventional and younger undergraduate
students and, as a consequence, probably make more
sacrifices to attend college, especially one that is
residential.

INTRODUCTION TO THE SCHOOL

Socialization to the values and norms of Ruskin
begins when the prospective student writes the required
2,000-word essay, completes the interview with the recruitment committee, and is notified of acceptance.
(See Appendix E for welcoming letter.) Socialization,
or introduction to his or her role in the school, is
hastened with the arrival in Oxford where the new students are met at the bus or railroad station by a committee of second-year students who represent the RSU.
They escort the new students to the school and ease

their adjustment to the surroundings during the first
day. In this capacity, the RSU acts as a bridge
between the social milieu the students have left and
the one they are entering. Fellow students who, like
themselves, have been active in the labor movement,
reassure the new students and relieve them of some of
the anxieties they feel on the first day of school.
In another capacity, the RSU acts as if it were the
collective bargaining agent of the students and the
school administration the employer.

Second-year students clue the newcomers into the
college regulations which include a "code of conduct,"
disciplinary procedures, and other rules and guides
that the college expects each student to follow. The
regulations, which also include the right of the student to be represented by the RSU, help the student
fit into the Ruskin pattern of student life. This
pattern includes the expectation that new students
will be guided by fairly high scholastic standards
and the recognition that they are adults with a strong
sense of their identity and views. All of this has
also been explained in the "Joining Instructions"
each student receives two months before arriving at
the school.

Part of the orientation process is the meeting
held the first evening of the first term. Here the
principal introduces the staff and tells the students
what they may expect during the first term. An
important aspect of the 1978 welcoming meeting that
I attended was the RSU president's speech to the students. He set the tone for the relationship between
staff and students by calling the principal by his
first name and facetiously informing the new students
that Ruskin had a "closed shop" and they were expected
to join the RSU. He concluded by announcing that the
credo of Ruskin students is "to eliminate injustices
in this world." After his remarks, a question period
was opened by the principal. The first question, more
a declaration, was the criticism directed against the
principal that there were not enough flats for married
students who had brought their spouses to Oxford with
them. Comments by the RSU speaker and the new students
indicated that they viewed the administration as adversaries, an attitude one might expect since the worker-
student is more prone than the conventional college
student to view college administrators and faculty as
adversaries.

The first week is devoted to orientation programs
that explain the courses and discuss the range of academic choices available. During the same week the
students make their "preliminary" selection of subjects
and courses. Each is also assigned an advisory tutor
who will counsel the student for the next two years and
a subject tutor who will be replaced each term as the
student's subjects of study change.

The schedule of the first week of the 1978 term
was a good example of how new students are introduced
to the school. New students met with the tutors on
Monday, the first day of the term. A social was held
the same evening after dinner. On Tuesday students
were given diagnostic exams that included tests in the
use of English. On the same day meetings were held
with the house tutor assigned to the student, with the
principal, and with the housekeepers. On Wednesday
the preliminary choice of courses and subjects for
which students registered earlier in the week began.
On Thursday the students were introduced to the Ruskin
library and Oxford University's Bodelian Library where
they registered. From 9:00 a.m. to 1:00 p.m. on Friday, there were two courses offered. On Saturday
second-year students took the first-year students on a
tour of Oxford. Although the new students were kept
busy, the college made certain that there was time for
recreation and relaxation. The warmth of the welcome
by both second-year students and the administrators
and faculty expressed the character of the social climate of Ruskin.

SOCIAL DIFFERENTIATION AMONG STUDENT GROUPS

Among the things about the Ruskin student body that
I observed early in the term was the development of groups
or social clusters. This social differentiation occurs
in part because students must make an early decision about
which diplomas they intend to study for. Those who are
studying for the same diploma tend to go to the same
classes, share similar hours, work on similar diploma
committees, prepare for the same tests, and share the
same tutors. They may even be paired for their tutorials.
In addition, they tend to share the same occupational
goals and spend their free time in the same recreational
social, and, frequently, political activities. All of

34

these characteristics may cause the students to share the
same or similar meanings, roles, and norms while at Ruskin.
    To test my own speculations about the group differ-
ences, I talked with the tutors, students, and former
students of Ruskin. The following analysis is basically
a heuristic device calculated to stimulate further investigation of how working-class adult students in long-
term residential colleges are socially differentiated.
    I found that I could consider the history, litera-
ture, and social studies majors (1970-79) as one group
and treat it as if its members were liberal arts majors.
This group is the largest, consisting of 49 percent of
the graduates, followed by labor studies with 28 percent,
social workers with 14 percent, and development studies
with 6 percent. In general there seems to be a hierarchy
of prestige that follows the same order. Each of the
four groups has differentiating characteristics.
    According to the tutors I interviewed, a higher
proportion of liberal arts students have gone on to
schools of higher education than have the students in
the other groups, which well might be expected. Perhaps
the most distinctive students in this group are those
who were awarded the literature diploma. Blumler quotes
a student who graduated in the 1950s and whose remarks indicated the attitude of literature students toward those
associated with the political left: "I shared a room
with one of the literature students and [they] seemed to
get along best with the apolitical lot. Perhaps they
felt superior to the political boys--a detached amuse-
ment in relation to them--and I was affected by this."[18]
In an informal conversation with four students almost
two decades later (October 1978), a labor studies student discussing the literature students told me: "We
don't feel comfortable with those studying for the
literature diploma. They seem to be a different lot
and don't associate with the labor people." None of
the other three students disagreed with this observation.
My own impression of the literature students is that
they were more urbane and more detached, more analytical, and had more intellectual interests than other
Ruskin students.
    The second largest of the four groups is made up
of the students in labor studies. This group includes
students interested in unions, politics, cooperatives,
and workers' education. Those who are the most conspicuous in the labor studies group are members of

left-wing groups or caucuses. They are by and large
the "missionaries" and the "career unionists." The
"missionaries" seek to recruit members of the labor
movement to the organizations to which they belong.
This may be the left wing of the Labour party, the
Communist party, or the Socialist Workers party, among
others. The "career unionists" seek to move ahead in
the labor movement by becoming influential among workers
and by acquiring full-time union jobs. The "missionaries" intend to enter or return to the labor movement
since they believe it to be the most progressive force
in society and the most capable of changing it, given
the proper program and leadership. Of the four groups,
the labor studies students have been the most critical
of the school's administration and tutors. Their basic
criticism has been that officials and tutors, with some
exceptions, are not sufficiently pro-labor or socialist.

The social work students make up the third largest
group. They are older, more businesslike, and more oc-
cupationally oriented than the students in the other
groups. They also have the lowest percentage of students who fail to qualify for diplomas. Their academic
courses plus practical training prepares them for place-
ment in social agencies immediately upon graduation,
and virtually all of them obtain jobs in social welfare
or community work. Because social work students must
pay weekly visits to local social agencies and are
placed in social agencies for several weeks, they are
not as active in the school as are members of the other
three groups and, as a consequence, they have less interaction with other Ruskin students.

The development studies students resemble the social
work students and the trade union careerists in that they
are geared to studying topics and materials that they hope
to apply to their respective concerns as soon as they
receive their Ruskin diplomas. Most of these students
were sent to Ruskin from third world countries* to learn
how to become effective administrators, planners, and
policy makers. Thus, the books and articles they were

---

*In the 1978-79 academic year, there were twenty students
from Barbadoes, Canada, Chile, Ethiopia, Fiji, Finland,
India, Israel, Kenya, Lesotho, Malawi, Malta, Mauritius,
Nigeria, Sierra Leone, St. Kitts-Nevis, Tanzania, and
Uganda (Ruskin College, Report and Accounts, 1979).

assigned dealt mainly with social, political, and economic change; peasants and peasant societies; and the dynamics of social groups. These writings were by authors such as Gunnar Myrdal, Immanual Wallerstein, Wilbert E. Moore, and Peter Worsley. Their immediate focus, however, was on learning to speak and write English correctly. The overseas students, at least initially, were assigned to classes as a group. There was little contact between them and the other students--with the exception of the left-wing students who actively sought them out.

Of the four groups, the students in labor studies contribute most to Ruskin as a whole and maintain a lively interest in, if not close ties to, the labor movement. Whether or not they are critical of the Labour party and the TUC and whether or not they plan to return to the union movement, these students stimulate debates about national issues and the policies of the TUC and the Labour party in classrooms, pubs, and in their rooms. Through these exchanges, a large number of students and tutors are drawn into a discussion of public issues and intellectual questions.

V.

The Social and Political Climate at Ruskin

The social climate of Ruskin is a mixture of values, hopes, and goals, some of which contradict each other. The acceptance of dissent in the school by the Governing Council, the officers of the school, and the tutors is an important factor in creating an atmosphere that facilitates the students' ability to think and question as well as to debate and to change or modify their views.

STUDENTS AND THE UNIONS

Although Ruskin acknowledges that it maintains close links with unions and other labor organizations, it has employed and continues to employ a number of tutors who are critical of the policies of labor leaders. Ruskin also recognizes the valuable contribution made to the student's intellectual development by the student debates that are stimulated by left-wing students. These debates cover such subjects as political and union policies, Marxism, socialism, and related questions. Radical literature and newspapers are occasionally sold on the premises of the school by students; leaflets advertising demonstrations and meetings of socialist, communist, and labor organizations appear on the bulletin boards. Meetings of such groups are held in the school building and given permission to do so by the RSU.

The Governing Council reflects the excellent relationship between Ruskin and labor. Despite the control of the school by unions through their membership on the council, they have accepted the students, political warts and all. For example, in 1976 when the then prime minister, James Callaghan, came to Ruskin to lay the foundation stone for a new residential wing, the students picketed in front

of the school demanding an increase in the national
educational budget. The Governing Council of Ruskin
made no comment.

The various principals of Ruskin have also played
a major role in the school's relationship with unions
as well as in shaping its social climate.[1] H. D. Hughes,
the sixth principal since Ruskin was founded (and who
retired in 1979 after twenty-nine years of service) was
no exception.* During his long tenure Hughes helped
develop an informal atmosphere by being accessible to
students and tutors. He has welcomed new ideas, and
maintained the school's connections with the TUC, the
Labour party, and other constituencies. In addition
he helped provide the school, its members and graduates,
with a sense of moral and intellectual continuity.

MISSIONARY ZEAL

Members of the Governing Council and some school
officials and tutors believe, as did the founders of
Ruskin, that students should return to their jobs and
to their communities and unions after graduating from
Ruskin. The school, however, does not impose its opinions on the students, most of whom hope to obtain jobs
in the labor movement and, if not, to go on to the university. The same students, motivated by missionary
zeal, may also feel guilty about these hopes because
they feel that they should return to their old jobs
and communities to help educate their former shopmates
and improve their communities. But, by the time the

---

*He is a former member of the House of Commons, president
of the WEA, and active in adult education. He served as
administrator, speaker, tutor, chief fund raiser, and
ambassador of the school. Hughes has also acted as an
advisor to the TUC and to the Labour party, served on
the Council of the Institute of Workers' Control, and
written a number of Fabian pamphlets and articles on continuing education. He considers himself a socialist; a
number of former students, however, especially members
of the left, consider him a "member of the labor
establishment."

second year is over, two-thirds of them have decided to
enter the university as a stepping stone to qualifying
for positions in unions or in public or nonprofit
organizations.

The social climate is in part reflected in the commitment of tutors to a service orientation. Behind
their impersonal and professional attitudes, according
to Pollins (interview, August 1978), they identify with
the labor movement and the aspirations of the students.
Most tutors harbor these feelings because, as Hammonds,
a Ruskin graduate, wrote, they have also gone through
residential schools for adults and know the fears and
hopes of the adult students. These feelings are shared
by educators active in adult education. "Humanitarian
and egalitarian impulses have always been an essential
part of adult education" and much more so, I would add,
in labor or workers' education.[2]

While Ruskin tutors may have a service orientation
toward their students, they do not necessarily accept
the role of missionary carrying the torch of learning to
the benighted student. For instance, when questioned
specifically about whether they believed the missionary
spirit exists among Ruskin tutors, some tutors indicated
that they were skeptical of the missionary role (interviews, November 1978). One of them said:

> I don't think that's probably likely.
> Perhaps I'm putting my head on the
> block but I think I'm a good deal less
> missionary-minded than when I first
> arrived here. Perhaps one or two of
> my colleagues are. I'm not missionary-
> minded in the sense that there's a kind
> of perhaps fanatical, even romantic
> drive within me....I think I do this
> because it's a job that needs to be
> done and done efficiently but I see it
> as more of an academic than a kind of
> religious mission in life.

Another tutor commented:

> The heroic period is over in workers'
> education. Most of the tutors see
> themselves as professionals, although
> they have their values.

40

Another said: "There are no missionaries left." And,
when asked whether he identified with the labor movement, one tutor responded:

> We all identify ourselves with the move-
> ment because that's part of being here.
> I don't mean that it's a formal require-
> ment because I would not be here unless
> I believed in it. I must admit that I
> am more skeptical than some of my col-
> leagues not just about the Labour party
> but about social action....I'm a kind of
> skeptical radical or perhaps a cynical
> radical. I'm very cynical about the
> possibilities of social change.

Paul Brodetsky, a tutor who answered the same question,
said:

> Nearly all my teaching life has been
> with workers. Although I am middle
> class myself, I've always had a strong
> identification with the labor movement.
> All the same, I enjoy teaching the sub-
> jects I do. If I had to choose be-
> tween teaching workers subjects that
> didn't particularly interest me and
> teaching nonworkers, undergraduates,
> for example, I think I would choose the
> latter. But I would rather teach with
> workers because the subject I teach is
> more meaningful with people who have
> had some experience already. If you
> want to characterize tutors as a whole,
> Fabian socialists would be the least
> inaccurate description. There are only
> a minority of tutors who are avowed
> Marxists. Sometimes the staff doesn't
> seem to have any very strong political
> or ideological views. Some have very
> pronounced and very clear ones.

Brodetsky's views were the most typical of the
comments volunteered by the tutors. He and most other
tutors were either members of the Labour party or among
its supporters, somewhat left of the center, formerly

41

more politically active, and now more academically
oriented. Of the minority of tutors who were radicals
the following remark by a tutor and former Ruskin student
(interview, October 1978) represented the more moderate
leftists in Ruskin, perhaps on their way to becoming
middle-of-the-roaders or Fabian socialists:

> Throughout my mature life...I have always
> been involved politically. Until 1978 I
> was a member of the Labour party and active
> within that as an educationalist, as an
> activist, as a secretary, as an organizer...
> on a voluntary basis, never paid for that
> kind of work and this is my most inactive
> period in the sense of political commitment.
> But it's still there....I consider myself
> a Marxist, a revolutionary, and therefore to
> the left of the Labour party, but having
> said that I cannot turn my back on the
> party because there's a hell of a lot of
> revolutionaries in the Labour party.

There was also a member of the Communist party and a Maoist
among the tutors who were associated with the left and very
popular with the students. The varying opinions held by
tutors are often unspoken assumptions, leading to different
approaches and different relationships with students.

STUDENT CULTURE

In schools like Ruskin with highly politicized students, the student culture mirrors the national debates
and political events of the times. Student discussions
and debates also reflect major differences between the
left and right within the Labour party and between the
various political sects. For example, Peter Rosenfeld,
a Ruskin graduate, who is chief educational officer of
the Union of Shop Distributive and Allied Workers, told
me (October 1978) that in the 1950s at Ruskin "there
were debates between Communists and Trotskyists and
also with Labour party students." He believed that
these debates contributed to the sophistication of the
students and their intellectual development:

I am not saying that they were particularly well developed or rational or
thoughtful but they certainly argued
fiercely and constantly in the student
body. But I must make it quite clear
that those were perhaps some of the
most enjoyable and pleasant aspects of
the college because they were not
vitriolic or unpleasant controversies.

Asked to comment cn whether the debates had any educational value, Rosenfeld responded:

Oh, undoubtedly, there is no question
about it. The activities of students
outside lectures, outside formal study,
sitting together, arguing over their
cup of tea for hours on end was and
still is one of the most formative influences of the college and cannot be
overstated.

Stan Shipley, a Labour party M. P. and former Ruskin
student, also thought the student culture, including conflicts between younger and older students, played a role
in educating all Ruskin students in 1968. He saw internal
debates as ultimately leading to an expansion of labor
courses, the introduction of democracy in Ruskin government, and greater participation in outside demonstrations
and protest meetings. These remarks were made at a symposium on "Ruskin College in the 1960s," led by three
former Ruskin students, November 17, 1978.

Another former Ruskin student, currently a tutor at
Ruskin, whom I questioned about the role of student culture in Ruskin, noted (interview, October 1978):

Ruskin is a mixture of the informal and
formal and I believe that the informal
discussions are equally valuable as the
formal discussions....The students' discussions go on until the small hours of
the night with two, three, sometimes ten
students discussing political attitudes,
certain topics, or philosophy of labor.

Still another tutor whom I asked to comment on the causes of debate replied (interview, October 1978):

> Committed Marxists. They are a minority
> of our population. They don't add a thing.
> They are more vocal and they are more
> easily heard. They stick to the same
> ideological point that they have been mak-
> ing consistently. I would say that the
> solid mass of students although not anti-
> pathetic to Marxism are not committed to
> it in quite the same way--and act as a
> kind of center of gravity. They help main-
> tain a source of balance.

Asked to describe the kind of students who make up the student body, he said:

> In effect you have three kinds of stu-
> dents coming to the college. Those who
> are on the older left, those who are in
> the New Left and who you might say believe
> in utopia. You have the hard center which
> I believe is the majority of students, the
> middle-of-the-roader, and also the oppor-
> tunists. If you like, we have the utopi-
> ans, the middle-of-the-roaders, and the
> hard opportunists, i.e., the self-
> improvers--who see Ruskin as simply
> another educational institution. The
> majority are silent.

He saw the various political sects, however, as dominating the student body. His position received support from a Trotskyist, a Ruskin student in 1966-68, who spoke in the symposium referred to earlier:

> Of course there were Labour party support-
> ers, leading unionists, C. P. groups,
> and two Trotskyists of which I was one.
> Ruskin always had selected students from
> across the political spectrum. A major-
> ity of the Ruskin students resented the
> changing life style of a minority of
> Ruskin students which was expressed in
> dress, smoking pot, and in other ways.

> The majority was quite respectable
> while the minority were younger, single,
> and into drugs. The majority regarded
> the minority as effeminate.

There appears to be some differences among graduates and tutors about the number of radicals and which radical group played a more prominent role in the school. What is clear, however, is that members of the left played a predominant role in shaping the student culture from the founding of the school until the present.

It is also clear that a major aspect of the student culture has been the intensive and extensive debates among students. The students I interviewed and those interviewed by other researchers have all acknowledged that the internal life of the school, especially the political debates, was extremely important for their intellectual growth.

While this kind of interaction might well occur outside the residential setting, it is evident from my experience that residential life provides an excellent medium for its growth. The report of the Russell Committee supports this conclusion. When the committee examined the importance of residential adult colleges, it concluded that "within the colleges themselves there has been the stimulus of cultural activities, and close contact with other students sharing similar aspirations and problems but drawn from all parts of the country and many other parts of the world."[3] The memoirs of an African worker recounting his Ruskin experience in 1948 illustrate this statement:

> The student body was a grand lot: English-
> men, Scotsmen, Welshmen, Irishmen, and
> Americans. How wonderfully we all mixed.
> Communists and fellow travellers seized
> every opportunity to discuss the grand
> millennium when the workers will rule
> the world. Socialists were always ad-
> vocating hastening slowly and so on.[4]

Another aspect of life in a residential college is that, compared to life at home, it is more interesting and pleasant. This is especially true of Ruskin because it is located in a city where the traditions and rites associated with Oxford University are still vigorously observed. In a

small university town like Oxford, it is possible to be
exposed to new ideas by interacting with Oxford students
from different regions of Great Britain and from overseas.[5]
Smith found that among his respondents, "contact with students of other colleges" ranked second among the activities that Ruskin graduates believed stimulated them intellectually during their stay at the college. Ranking first
was intellectual stimulation by fellow students; ranking
third was intellectual stimulation by members of radical
or single-issue organizations ranging from the Socialist
Workers party to antipollution groups.[6]

Those who completed their studies at Ruskin said it
was pleasant being away from the shop, having different
and flexible hours, meeting new people, and indulging in
the role of student. Haffner, who was once a Ruskin student, summed up the reaction of many students: "It was
the best two years of my life" (interview, October 1978).

The pleasantness of life at Ruskin, however, is said
to be a contrast with the reception many students have
received when visiting their friends, former shopmates,
and union colleagues between terms or after receiving
their diplomas. They were accused of having "lost all
interest in the struggles of their old workmates."[7] Perhaps the criticism of Jack Jones,* general secretary of
the Transport and General Workers Union, summarized the
opinions of a number of unionists and others, at least
during the 1920s and earlier:

> We have had the experience of men who
> have gone to Ruskin College dressed
> up as workmen who have come back with
> halos, dressed in plus fours, and
> immediately wanting to be general
> secretary of their union and the very
> people who have not had the education,
> the men who have learned all they know
> in the workshop, have paid the money
> to keep these people in college, away
> from the surroundings of the class to
> which they belong.[8]

---

*The Jack Jones of the 1920s is not to be confused with Jack
Jones, general secretary of the Transport and General Workers
Union (TGWU) in 1978.

A similar reaction was reported by John Lowe in the early
1960s who suggested that "this may be one reason why so
many of the students seek professional outlets at the end
of their course."[9] The reaction of the students once they
attend school suggests a "push-pull" scheme for interpret-
ing their behavior: the "push" of their former shopmates
makes it difficult for them to return to their former
jobs and the "pull" of their newly acquired education moti-
vates them to seek new goals and new jobs.

The comments scattered through the literature as well
as those made to me in the interviews at Ruskin convey
rather accurately the role of the student culture in creating the social and political climate of Ruskin. Student
culture strongly influences the development of the students,
their level of sophistication, and their aspirations. In
turn, the character of the student culture is affected by
the liberal climate of Ruskin--which is influenced by its
tutors, its administrators, and its students--and by the
fact that the interplay of these factors is facilitated
in the residential setting.

VI.

Residential Education and the Process of Change

The Russell Committee found that long-term residential colleges "have a remarkable record of finding men and women from unpromising backgrounds and developing their intellectual capacities and personalities so that they have gone on to make important contributions to society."[1] What is there about the long-term residential adult college that enables students with "unpromising backgrounds" to make "important contributions to society," despite the difficulties and problems of changing from one style of life to another?

An entrant who wishes to become an integral part of a long-term residential college for adults has to learn its patterns of behavior, assumptions, and norms. In doing so, he or she initiates a process that may have a significant effect on self-image, involvement, values, and accomplishments. This process is influenced by the social as well as the physical distance between the old environment and the new one. In commenting on this point, the Russell Committee pointed out:

> Full-time study makes sustained intel-
> lectual demands and, when combined with
> individual tuition and the full life of
> the college, produces much more rapid
> intellectual growth than is possible
> under conditions of part-time study.
> None of this would be within reach of,
> for example, students from deprived
> backgrounds without the change of en-
> vironment and the temporary release
> from voluntary activities and family
> responsibilities that a residential
> college offers. The greater, however,

the need for removal from home and
family to achieve educational progress,
the greater is likely to be the cultural
distance between the student and his
home as his course develops.[2]

THE ADULT STUDENT AND SELF-IMAGE

There is consensus among adult educators that some
of the major goals of adult education are education for
self-discovery and self-fulfillment and for bringing
about personal and social change. There are, of course,
many ways of achieving social change. As Vrooman formu-
lated it, the role of education is "methodically and
scientifically to possess the world, to refashion it,
and co-operate with the power behind evolution in making
it the joyous abode of, if not a perfected humanity, at
least a humanity earnestly and rationally striving towards perfection."[3] While many Ruskin students, past
and present, would disagree with the formulation of the
statement, they would agree with the substance of it.
Many Ruskin students, as I noted earlier, have been
attracted to the school to gain the knowledge and skills
they believe necessary to liberate mankind from the
evils of capitalism by erecting a new socialist society.

In the process of learning how to refashion the
world, Ruskin students themselves may be refashioned in
unanticipated ways. Blumler's study shows that some
graduates become more objective, less committed, and
more skeptical of the labor movement, while other graduates may move in the opposite direction. Many may go
through a "crisis of identity," according to Pollins,
who has taught at Ruskin for almost two decades, because they want "to retain their connection with their
roots or their commitment to trade unions or political
parties or--in a rather general sense--with their class."
The entrants, he goes on to say, believe they may lose
their connections with the working class if they continue on to higher education. The resulting dilemma is:
"Should they go back to their jobs? Should they go on
to university? Can they get back into the trade union
movement? These tensions inevitably arise."[4]

There may be other causes of the identity crisis.
Some students arrive at Ruskin uncertain of their
status, uncertain of their ability to meet the academic

requirements of the school, and uncertain as to whether they made the wisest decision in entering Ruskin. Students may also feel relatively deprived. They have left a union or shop where they exercised leadership and influence; they were respected and recognized for their achievements. The identity crisis may be a product of the new knowledge and life style that conflicts with previous knowledge and life style. In short, there is the conflict between an emerging identity and a precariously based old one.

If the student survives the identity crisis and acquires the attitudes, skills, and knowledge associated with academic work, these achievements are evidence that he or she can cope with the expectations of the school and with the problem of being away from home. This reconciliation may occur at the end of the first year when the student has had an adequate period to test academic capabilities and the ability to live in a residential college. During this phase of the student's development, he or she builds the foundation on which self-confidence and self-assurance eventually rest. A not uncommon comment is that of a Ruskin graduate who increased his "knowledge, ability, and confidence." He said, "Overall my impression is one of a period of tremendous stimulation--both from the academic and social side of Ruskin life. Clearly, it has had a marked effect upon my life....I honestly think I owe a debt here which I can never repay."[5] Vernon Merritt, the president of the RSU, a member of the left and a former accountant, noted in an interview (October 1978) that his ability to express himself had been sharpened, and he added "I have been able to extend my intellectual abilities as well. I took a course in socialism to test my own beliefs and emerged with a broader perspective and deeper analytical approach to political questions. I have the satisfaction of being respected by students and tutorial staff as well."

Smith found that over one-third of his sample of Ruskin graduates claimed that their experience at the college had given them "confidence, the ability to research and present facts." Four years later, Pollins, who also commented on the growth of self-confidence among Ruskin students, pointed out that "the great majority of students adapt and at some point in their college career achieve a break-through. They become self-confident; they can handle the various subjects with ease; they can write better; they are aware of problems of logical argument and of the validity of empirical data." Similar findings can be deduced from the study by Ruskin itself of the accomplishments of students with the least formal schooling. This study found that "on the whole the students with the least record of school education and the lowest pre-College socio-economic status did at least as well as those who had attended grammar schools or who entered College from clerical work or higher forms of occupation."[6]

If the various studies we have cited are fairly accurate, it may be reasonably inferred that there have been changes in the self-image of Ruskin students as a result of an increase in their esteem, confidence, and respect they have for themselves.

New Involvements

The change in self-image of the student is in part a result of new involvements. Upon entering the school the adult worker acquires the role of student and in this capacity interacts with at least three major groups: tutors, co-students, and other students in the city of Oxford, mainly from Oxford University. Introduction to each of these groups may facilitate reception of new ideas and new values by the student and may lead to changes in self-image.

The student's relationship with the tutor has aspects of superordination-subordination and is based on the professional and positional authority of the tutor. The tutor's aim is to prepare the student to be intellectually independent. But the student, in the early phase of development, often resents the authority of the tutor and the school administration; he or she feels uprooted, anomic, and faces the threat of once again failing as a student. For the most part, tutors understand these feelings. One tutor, a former Ruskin student, wrote about his early days at Ruskin: "We know the feeling of apprehension, of facing up to further stigmatization as a 'failure.'"[7]

Pollins implies, however, that despite the similarity of their social origins, political ideologies, and union backgrounds, tutors are not necessarily sympathetic to students' morale problems. Neither the literature nor my interviews with tutors indicated that they were highly involved with the emotional lives of their students. They tended to keep students at arm's length if only to protect

the ability to evaluate their work objectively. The
tutors' concern for the students is not expressed in
a personal or informal manner but rather in the meticulous care with which they prepare their subject matter
and their criticisms and assessments of the students'
work. The tutors also show their concern in their determi-
nation that the students acquire the academic virtues.
In general, as Pollins points out, the obligation of
tutors "to respond to the needs of their adult students
is not as straightforward as it sometimes appears." The
needs of students are diverse and they change as they
become more involved with their studies.[8]

The school has tried to meet the emotional needs of
the students by separating the tutors' instructional
responsibilities from their morale responsibilities and
by allowing the students to select a tutor who will be
their advisor during their stay at Ruskin. But the most
effective stabilizing force for the students is their
peer group.

The students provide emotional support for each other
and use the RSU as a forum for protesting methods of evaluation of students, residential problems, and administrative
decisions. They raise their morale by participating in
demonstrations against, for example, discrimination, the
"Nazi-front," and "nukes."[9] Most of all, they relieve
their strains by commiserating with one another over a
beer or in "bitch" sessions. In the process, they demonstrate that they are not just students, but individuals
who are active and skillful in other statuses.

Mutual support and the protest demonstrations reduce
the strain students feel and mask the relationship between them and the school. As a result, the desired
academic relationship between tutor and student is pre-
served. At the same time, the encounters of Ruskin students with Oxford students introduce them to a broader
range of personalities than they have been accustomed to
meeting. In carrying on polemics with Oxford students,
socializing with them in pubs, and meeting them in classes,
they become more cosmopolitan and sophisticated.

Student culture then, at Ruskin and elsewhere, is the
result of norms and values of the individuals who share
similar roles, perspectives, and interests as students.
Such norms and values include the acceptance of attitudes
and patterns of behavior necessary to meet the requirements
of a college or university. Student culture also includes
an ideology that justifies the students' efforts to protect

their own interests, self-esteem, and outlook. This ideology relieves them of the strain they endure as students and the strain they feel as they change in response to the ideas and behavior of teachers and co-students. In sum, the student culture makes it possible for students to pass from the role of worker to student and then to professional.

New Values

As the students begin to find life in the school more comfortable and stimulating than life at the work-site, they begin to orient to the idea of the college education and of eventually getting full-time jobs that are more congruent with their new outlook. One student who was quoted by Smith said, "life at Ruskin taught me that the 9-to-5 syndrome was not inevitable." This reaction was confirmed in my discussion with students. As students internalize academic standards, they become more critical, logical, and intellectual. Their perception of themselves and of those with whom they interact changes, and their view of what they expect in a job, a political party, and a union is altered. In effect, their new outlook and new involvements modify, as Blumler says, the "whole code by which [they] interpret life as it impinges on them from day-to-day."[10]

New Accomplishments

The new self-image, new involvements, and new values that are shaped by the experiences at Ruskin are in part responsible for the accomplishments of Ruskin graduates. Quite clearly, getting a Ruskin diploma is one measure of intellectual achievement and of the ability to overcome difficult and unfamiliar problems that confronted them as students. Another measure of accomplishment is the kind of jobs Ruskin graduates--even those who do not go on to university--accept compared to jobs they held before entering Ruskin.

Even before graduation, the students become aware of the type of jobs they might qualify for and try to contact leading union officials or officials of organizations devoted to adult or workers' education or social work. The difficulty of obtaining a job in accord with the new

53

abilities of the student is eased by the reputation of Ruskin. Ruskin found that the background of its graduates is highly regarded by the WEA, extramural departments of universities, and trade unions that have employed Ruskin graduates as tutors or staff members. Other factors contributing to the ability ot Ruskin students to obtain such jobs are the "enhanced self-confidence" Blumler described and their part-time teaching experience at Ruskin. It is not surprising that many graduates are employed as professionals or semiprofessionals by service organizations and that Smith found as did Blumler that only a small percent of Ruskin graduates have "returned to their old jobs or jobs of a similar nature."[11]

Career patterns of Ruskin graduates indicate that a significant number of them have important jobs at all levels in a number of professions. A study by Sir Arthur Salter, M.P., of positions held by Ruskin graduates in the 1930s reported that in addition to jobs in unions they held twenty-one jobs in higher education, twenty in social service, twenty in welfare, nineteen in cooperatives, seventeen in Parliament (Labour M.P.'s), six in journalism, four in civil service, one in business, and eight or more in local government authorities.[12] Many of the jobs held by the graduates were near the top of the hierarchy in their field. One graduate, for example, was the general secretary of the TUC, another was the editor of a newspaper, and a third was a professor.

Ruskin, in its evidence to the Donovan Committee (Royal Commission on Trade Unions and Employers' Associations), listed sixty-nine full-time union posts and sixty-seven industrial relations posts held by former students in the years between 1960 and 1965.[13] Table 1 is a comparison of the high status occupations of 143 Ruskin graduates from 1946 through 1957 and 525 graduates from 1970 through 1979. The graduates in both groups are clustered in three occupational categories: professional and semiprofessional; labor movement, staff and officials; and public employment, executive and higher. Eighty-two percent of the 1946-57 graduates and 91 percent of the 1970-79 graduates held jobs in these three categories. There was a decrease from 14 percent in 1945-57 to 5 percent in 1970-79 of graduates in high status jobs in private industry and commerce.*

THE ORGANIZATION AND THE PROCESS OF CHANGE

The accomplishments of Ruskin students and the changes they perceive in themselves are part of a process that frequently occurs when an individual enters a complex organization. If the organization is to survive it must be able to socialize its new members to its values, norms, and practices. As Caplow put it, "the new man must be fitted into the status order, the interaction network, and the activities of the organization, while simultaneously acquiring the appropriate sentiments for each type of participation." In effect, the entrant is required by the organization to "acquire...a new self-image,...new involvements,... new values and...new accomplishments."[14]

The school, as an organization, is not exempt from this basic process if it is to meet its goals, one of which is to prepare the student to become a successful candidate for graduation. On the other hand, the school is unlike, for example, a typical profit-making organization, since the goals of the school are broader and its range and scope more comprehensive. In addition, its effect on its members is more permanent. This is especially true of schools whose administration and faculty are committed to personal goals that include changing or modifying the social order. In the process, the school influences the values and behavior as well as the self-image and accomplishments of the student.

---

*Some of the distinguished graduates, in addition to those noted in the introductory section, are Allan Fox, novelist; Ben Roberts, a leading writer in industrial and labor relations; George Woodcock, former general secretary of the TUC; and the late Tom Mboya, once a leading figure in Kenya. In his book, Freedom and After (London: Andre Deutsch, 1946, p. 58), Mboya wrote that his experiences at Ruskin in 1955 gave him more confidence in himself, taught him to read books as a source of his knowledge, and stimulated him "to take part in intellectual discussions, sometimes of a very provocative nature."

Table 1: Comparison of High-Status Occupations of Ruskin
Graduates for Two Periods, 1946–57 and 1970–79

Occupational field	1946–57			1970–79		
	#	% of category	% of total	#	% of category	% of total
PROFESSIONAL AND SEMIPROFESSIONAL	60	100	42	225	100	43
School teaching	27	45		17	8	
Social work	17	28		64	28	
University and College teaching and research	13	22		144	64	
Other	3	5		–	–	
LABOR MOVEMENT, STAFF AND OFFICIALS	36	99 (rounding)	25	164	100	31
Union	21	58		91	55	
Political	4	11		42	26	
Cooperative Movement	3	8		6	4	
Adult or Workers' Education	8	22		25	15	
PUBLIC EMPLOYMENT, EXECUTIVE AND HIGHER	22	100	15	87	100	17
Nationalization	9	41		23	26	
Civil Service	7	31		32	37	
Local Government and Public Corporation	6	28		32	37	
PRIVATE INDUSTRY AND COMMERCE	20	–	14	28	–	5
MISCELLANEOUS	5	–	4	21	–	4
Total	143		100	525		100

Source: The 1946–57 data are from Blumler, "The Effects of
Long-Term Residential Adult Education," p. 51, table 8, which
I have modified by transferring teachers in "Further" and
"Technical" colleges from his category of "School Teaching"
to "University and College Teaching and Research." The 1970–79
data have been compiled from Ruskin's Report and Accounts.

In brief, although Ruskin owes its reputation for
academic excellence in part to the cooperation of Oxford University, it also owes its reputation to students
who are politically oriented and who seek admittance to
Ruskin in the hope that they will be accepted by Oxford
or another university. Certainly, by the end of the
two-year stay at Ruskin, status aspirations and interaction with Oxford students and traditions have served
as motivators for enrolling in Oxford or, if not Oxford, in other universities.

HIGHER EDUCATION AND STATUS

The desire for higher status and economic security
is often the reason students enter schools of higher
education including Ruskin. Analytically, however,
status and economic security may be treated as separate
variables, just as life style is treated separately
from life chances. Melvin M. Tumin, for example, sub-
sumes life style under status and life chances under
class and says that status and class may be considered
as separate "ladders" for achieving wealth or distinction. This is particularly true in Britain where, as
W. G. Runciman writes, "distinctions of status are
deep rooted, pervasive and readily visible." And
status is expressed "in such attributes as education,
accent, style of dress and...type of job." Max Weber
observed that "in content, status honor is normally
expressed by the fact that above all else a specific
style of life can be expected from all those who wish
to belong to the circle." Addressing himself specifically to education, he noted that "the development of
the diploma from universities, and business and engineering colleges, and the universal clamor for the
creation of educational certificates in all fields
make for the formation of a privileged stratum in
bureaus and in offices." Applying the constructs
of Weber and others to Great Britain, Runciman noted
that although the worker had achieved some "measure
of economic equality with reference to the lower-
middle class, this was largely a separate matter from
the recognition by the strata above him of his equal
status as a 'gentleman.'"[15]

These comments provide a backdrop for understanding the role that the desire for higher status plays

in impelling workers to seek higher education. This
aspiration is understandable, particularly in a country
where trade union leaders are honored by the aristocracy with titles and where nearly 25 percent of the
workers vote for the Conservative party, many out of
deference to the status, traditions, and "hereditary
institutions" associated with many of its members.[16]
But, although earning a university degree is an important way of achieving higher status, it does not follow
that every Ruskin graduate who goes on to the university does so to become a member of the upper class.
Rather, many enter the university because they want a
job in the union or to serve the working class or the
commonweal. High status is thrust upon the university
graduates because of their achievement and new role,
especially by members of the working class who have
been deprived of a university education.

Adult residential college students in Great Britain
seek an education for various reasons: in part to raise
their status, in part to help the working class, and in
part to reduce ambivalent feelings about self and job.
In their study, Earl Hopper and Marilyn Osborn described
adult workers who, because of their experience and educational background "as well as their ambivalent self-
identifications and generally low self-esteem,...are
in marginal situations within their status groups and
occupational roles." As a result, they have "returned
to formal education in an effort to reduce their feelings of relative deprivation."[17]

The literature about British adult working-class
students abounds with remarks about style of life, ad-
monitions not to leave one's class, and comments about
deferential workers. And, throughout the history of
Ruskin College, for example, its students have had a
"love/hate" relationship with Oxford University--sus-
picious of its class nature and its privileged position, yet, many wanting to become Oxford students.
One aspect of the relationship is noted by William W.
Craik, one of the Ruskin students who left Ruskin to
launch the Central Labour College. He quoted from a
newspaper to express how he and others felt in the
early 1900s about working-class students who left their
"class": "The Oxford student of humble origin too often
passes out of the world from which he sprang--'looks in
the Clouds, scorning the base degrees By which he did
ascend.'"[18] The tradition left by earlier students is

still strong at Ruskin even if it is often honored more
in the breach than in its observance. In fact, the
fear of working-class students becoming turncoats after
entering schools of higher learning is implied in the
following comment from A. Burchardt in 1974.

> I would hope that, with luck, one might
> retain the working-class contacts, culture
> and aspirations of the students and avoid
> the personal and social/class disorienta-
> tion that affects students at existing
> residential adult education colleges,
> while at the same time providing the most
> powerful of analytical tools for criti-
> cally examining major aspects of our
> society.[19]

Notwithstanding their disdain, increasing numbers
of students are entering universities, including Oxford. Some estimate of the number is indicated by
comments by H. D. Hughes noting that over 75 percent
of the 1978 graduates were accepted by universities
as compared to nearly 25 percent who were accepted in
1959. One important reason more students have gone on
to university has been the greater demand from unions.
They and the WEA branches, local educational authorities, and the Labour party have created a labor market
for working-class university graduates. In fact,
Stanley Pierson observed that as early as 1899 the concern for the larger responsibilities of citizenship
was a major reason for the founding of Ruskin. He
said, "The growing Socialist and labor representation
on local governing bodies also revealed that the
'supply of suitable men' for the kind of work was
'becoming exhausted.'"[20] Even at that time, few workers
could achieve the skills necessary to meet the complex
tasks that these jobs demanded without training at a
school of higher education. While the reason for
accepting a job in any one of these areas was undoubtedly economic, another major reason, as we have indicated, was that of achieving higher status.

Ruskin graduates who have been accepted by Oxford
have prepared for the event--even if indirectly--by
enrolling in Ruskin's Oxford University Special Diploma in Social Studies. In this course, they are brought
closer to Oxford students by sharing lectures with them

at the university and socializing with them outside
of class. Thus, they are sensitized to what is
expected of students entering Oxford, which, in
turn, may facilitate their admission to Oxford.
There are probably more Ruskin graduates who have
entered Oxford than have entered any other single
university in Great Britain.[21]

External examiners who are also Oxford dons
become sources for recommendations for those entering Oxford and other universities.[22] One incentive
for entering Oxford or other universities has been
the allocation, in effect, of credit for the work at
Ruskin. These credits permit the Ruskin graduate to
study for two years instead of three years to earn
a bachelor's degree or to enter an honors-degree
program.

The Russell Committee found that many universities and other organizations of higher learning have
been recognizing a diploma awarded by long-term residential adult colleges as qualification "for admission
and in a growing number of cases for exemption from
part of a degree course." Their report called on all
universities and organizations of higher learning to
extend credit and recognition to holders of diplomas
from residential adult colleges.[23]

To sum up, Ruskin has an important impact on the
student's self-image, involvements, values, and
accomplishments. New friends and relationships, new
jobs, more poise and new self-confidence, new achievements and the desire to occupy more interesting roles
are developed and stimulated by Ruskin, acting in part
as a mediating agency of the larger social system.

VII.

Comparison of Ruskin with Other Labor Colleges

A comparison of Ruskin with other residential adult colleges in Great Britain permits a clearer understanding of how an adult college devoted primarily to the education of unionists differs from a college devoted to general adult education. Moreover, a comparison of adult labor education on a college level in the United States with that in Great Britain may lead to a better understanding of how philosophical and structural differences, especially between the two labor movements, affect the education of organized workers. Finally, because a comparison study involves more organizations and a larger population, it provides a way to refine the analysis of the subject under study and to make applications from the findings.

ADULT RESIDENTIAL COLLEGES IN GREAT BRITAIN

Throughout the relevant literature, the phrase "long-term residential adult college" is used to describe Ruskin and other British residential colleges. The report of the Russell Committee, for example, describes them as being "long-term residential colleges providing courses of liberal adult education of one or two years' duration." Ruskin, in the Oxford Prospectus, describes itself as a "residential college for adult education open to men and women students....It holds as its continuing aim the provision of higher education for working men and women." The other residential colleges--Co-operative (1919), Hillcroft (1920), Plater, formerly Catholic Workers College (1921), Coleg Harlech (1927), and New-battle Abbey (1937)--use similar descriptions in publicizing their programs. Two other long-term residential

colleges for adults, Fircroft (1909) and Northern (1978),
use similar descriptions.* Alice Cook and Agnes Douty,
however, have characterized Ruskin, Fircroft, Hillcroft,
Newbattle Abbey, and Coleg Harlech as labor colleges, and
although a number of the colleges described here might
easily be called labor colleges, I will follow British
convention and refer to them as long-term adult residential colleges.[1]

As table 2 indicates, Ruskin shares a number of
characteristics with the other colleges: (1) all the
schools are small; (2) the average age of the students
ranges from twenty-six for Coleg Harlech to thirty for
Ruskin and Hillcroft; (3) Ruskin, Plater, and Coleg
Harlech give preference to early school leavers; (4)
at least 50 percent of the students admitted are manual
workers, although Ruskin probably enrolls more skilled
workers than the other schools; and (5) with the possible
exception of Newbattle Abbey, all the schools receive
grants from the Department of Education and Science,
local educational authorities, or their Welsh and Scot-
tish equivalent. Except for Hillcroft, a women's college, all the schools welcome male and female students
although the coeducational schools have problems recruiting women. All of the colleges seek students
who have been active in civic or volunteer activities
and students from the third world who wish to learn
how to make more effective contributions to the development of their countries.

With the exception of Co-operative College, all
schools have both one- and two-year programs. In addition, all the colleges offer liberal-arts curriculum
modified by their special interests: religion, cooperatives, regionalism, nationalism, or labor. Most
of the teaching is done by full-time staff. Three of
the schools use the Oxbridge tutorial method. None
offers credit for courses that can be applied toward
earning a university degree. Some universities, including Oxford, however, do recognize their diplomas
by excusing graduates of the six colleges from certain

---

*They are, however, not included in this study because
Northern was launched only about two years ago and Fircroft has only recently reopened after being closed for
several years as a result of a dispute between the
school administration on one side and the faculty and
students on the other.

Table 2: Comparison of Selected Characteristics of Six Long-Term Adult Residential Colleges

Characteristics	Ruskin College	Co-opera-tive College	Hillcroft College	Plater College	Coleg Harlech College	Newbattle Abbey College
Year of origin	1899	1919	1920	1921	1927	1937
No. of students	176	77	68	69	131	70
Basic method of teaching	tutorial	classes	classes	tutorial	tutorial	?
Average age of students	30	28	30	28	26	29
Recruits mainly early school leavers	yes	no	no	yes	yes	?
Recruits mainly manual workers	yes	yes	no	yes	yes	yes
Orientation of school	union	coop	women	religious	regional	regional
Grants from the DES (1970-71)[a]	$168,000	$13,000	$53,000	$53,000	$140,000	?

Sources: Russell Report, pp. 44 and 88; Ruskin College, Annual Report, 31 July 1979; Coleg Harlech, Fiftieth Annual Report, 1976-77; Hillcroft College, Annual Report 1976-77; Plater College, Annual Report, 1976-77; Newbattle Abbey, Annual Report of the Executive Committee for 1975-76; National Co-operative Education Association, Report of Education Executive, 1977.

[a]By 1980, the grants had become nearly twice as large.

63

courses or by placing them in honors classes. (Representatives of the colleges have been requesting for some time that credit for the studies leading to a diploma be extended to their graduates when they enroll in universities.) Five of the six colleges are in or near university towns where their students are exposed to new ideas, new styles of life, new circles, and new aspirations.[2] All the schools have students with union backgrounds and the curricula all include union studies or industrial relations courses. Finally, the colleges share a commitment to provide working-class adults, particularly those active in the labor movement, with a second chance to obtain a higher education.

There are several major differences between Ruskin and the other colleges. Although they all train their students for both labor leadership and entrance to universities, Ruskin stresses the former and the other five colleges stress the latter. Only Ruskin offers a diploma in labor studies. In addition, Ruskin has much closer ties with union officials and their interest in the school contributes to a social climate in which students, faculty, and administrators perceive the school as part of the labor movement, sharing in its defeats and triumphs. Consequently, Ruskin students are more attuned to what is required for employment and participation in the labor movement. The union movement's close ties with Ruskin are a source of students and a source of jobs for students when they graduate from Ruskin or from a university. Moreover, a large number of unions send their top officials to Ruskin to attend special one- or two-week programs. Many labor organizations also use Ruskin's facilities for their summer schools and other activities. Ruskin students, therefore, have more opportunities than the students of the other schools to meet with labor officials and obtain information about jobs in the labor movement.

There are other important differences. For example, Ruskin is the only one of the six colleges where trade union officers make up at least four-fifths of the Governing Council. Ruskin also has a much higher percentage of students who were union stewards. More of its graduates enter universities and are more likely to be accepted by Oxford and Cambridge. Ruskin graduates, compared to those of other colleges, have made more changes in their cultural activities, in the books and newspapers they read, in the status of their jobs, and in the friends and colleagues they associate with.[3]

The findings of Blumler, the Russell Committee, and other more recent studies make it clear that the six colleges have earned the respect of many interested parties and organizations for their contribution to the educationally "deprived." The findings of my study suggest, however, that there are important distinctions between Ruskin and the five other colleges; these distinctions are reflected in the nature of their students. Ruskin students, unlike the students at the five other colleges, are selected from a national pool of candidates irrespective of sex, region, or religion. In addition, most Ruskin students have a background of activity in working-class parties where their values and ideas were shaped and stimulated and in unions where their leadership skills were developed. Thus, students entering Ruskin are usually highly motivated and ready to challenge the opinions of peers and tutors as well as to coalesce with their peers into a well-knit student group that contributes to the culture and traditions of Ruskin.

WORKERS' EDUCATION IN GREAT BRITAIN AND THE UNITED STATES

Workers' education and labor colleges in Great Britain and the United States can be said to have had common roots during the social ferment of the nineteenth century. In Great Britain, union leaders and members accepted the ideas and values associated with a nonconformist religious tradition, Christian socialism, Fabianism, and a British-influenced Marxism. These views stemmed from the impact of the industrial revolution, which left a profound sense of class antagonism between workers on the one side and the landed aristocracy, corporations, and state on the other. This legacy was reinforced by the unyielding opposition of the Conservative party to the rights and interests of workers and working-class organizations. As a consequence, the labor movement became socialist and struggled to change the social order. Workers' education took root in this soil and was supported by the TUC and a number of its major national affiliates.

Workers' education in Great Britain from its beginning and for most of its existence has been characterized by an emphasis on education for changing the social order. It has been sponsored by friendly but independent voluntary organizations and designed for the individual

worker recruited directly by the organization involved.
The leaders of the union movement, preoccupied with
economics and political struggles, were for the most
part pleased to leave education to the organizations
that would educate workers so they could become econ-
omically and politically literate and work for social
emancipation. British workers' education, including
labor colleges, stressed social science, a broad
education, and participation by the workers in national affairs and in the union movement. It also encouraged the intellectual growth of the individual worker
and maintained close connections with the labor movement.

Until the 1890s, the American labor movement resembled the British labor movement insofar as it organized mostly skilled workers, emphasized voluntarism,
and stressed winning economic gains for the workers
it represented. And, although the American labor
movement remained comparatively uninfluential in
national, social, and political matters, its leadership as described by Cook and Douty "responded to
the crusades of the social reformers...who saw education as a way up for the masses of American workers."[4]

The convergence of British and American notions
of social reform during this period is exemplified
by the two American reformers, Walter Vrooman and
Charles Beard, who founded Ruskin College in Great
Britain and several similar instituions for workers
in the United States, some of which were also named
for the English reformer, John Ruskin. Similarities
between the two diminished when British unions began
to organize workers irrespective of trade, industry,
or skill and became the major support of the Labour
party, which they helped found. American labor
unions remained craft oriented and were more conservative.[5] In short, while the leaders of the British
labor movement sought to change the social order,
the leaders of the American union movement supported
the social order with some modifications. The notable
exception to this approach in the United States was
the support of workers' education in the early 1900s
by the socialist-influenced unions like the International Ladies Garment Workers Union, Amalgamated
Clothing Workers Union, and United Mineworkers Union.

In 1921, with the organization of the Workers
Education Bureau and the founding of Brookwood Labor

College and other labor colleges in the United States,
similarities with British workers' education appeared.
However, the American Federation of Labor (AFL) took
over the control of the Workers Education Bureau in
1929 and withdrew its support of Brookwood and the
other labor colleges launched by Brookwood graduates.
In relation to the withdrawal of support by the AFL,
James W. Robinson noted that "the distaste of U.S.
trade union leaders for direct political action designed to change the fundamental nature of the economy
made untenable the continued existence of workers' education programs such as Brookwood or the Rand School
[established in New York City in 1906 by the Socialist
party]."[6]

   With the withdrawal of AFL support, workers' education in the United States was dormant for almost a
decade. It was succeeded by "labor education" in response to the growth of the American labor movement,
especially the Congress of Industrial Organizations
(CIO), and from the impetus given the AFL and the CIO
from laws passed under the New Deal. The resulting
increase in collective bargaining agreements and the
number of local unions created a need for technical
training. Labor education was introduced as a tool
for training unionists in their roles as stewards,
business agents, and organizers.[7]

   Workers' education and labor education differed
in a number of respects. Whereas workers' education
stressed social science and cultural development,
labor education stressed "how to be a steward" and
other "tool" courses. Whereas workers were recruited
for workers' educational organizations on an individual
basis, they were recruited for labor education courses
through the unions. While workers' education was carried on by voluntary organizations and financed in the
main by private individuals and institutions, labor
education was financed in the late 1930s by the federal
government and later by state legislatures and the
unions themselves. And finally, whereas the courses
in workers' education often were for a year and in
residential labor colleges for two years, labor education courses generally were for six to eight weeks
with one ninety-minute session a week.

   During the 1960s, some convergence of the two
systems occurred. In the 1960s the TUC succeeded in
sponsoring on a broad scale in Great Britain basic

"role" education, the equivalent of the American "tool"
courses. At about the same time, American labor educators began to sponsor long-term labor studies courses
that resembled in breadth, variety, and complexity
the courses offered by Ruskin. Thus, Robinson noted,
"by 1965 the traditional characteristics of the programs in the two nations had become almost totally
reversed."[8]

Whatever the changes, disagreements among faculty
members (or tutors) of each country have persisted over
curricula, procedures for evaluating students, academic goals, and the relationship of their schools to
the labor movement. Differences on these and other
matters are not surprising since there is no consensus
among labor educators on the broad objectives of
labor education.[9] Perhaps the only consensus is that
union-supported or union-sponsored programs offered by
colleges and universities and attended by union members--
especially union activists--for college credit may be
loosely called labor studies.

LABOR STUDIES IN THE UNITED STATES:
SOME COMPARISONS WITH RUSKIN

Most labor studies programs are in university extension units, state colleges, or community colleges. They
offer a major in labor studies to union members, and
anyone else interested in the program. Students earn
credit toward either bachelor's or associate degrees.
A few programs offer credit for labor studies in cooperation with another school that awards the degrees.[10] In
a broad sense, these programs may be viewed as schools
on their way to becoming "labor colleges," and, within
that perspective, it is useful to compare them with
labor colleges such as Ruskin.

In 1975 at least forty-three American universities
or colleges offered certificate or degree courses roughly equivalent to Ruskin's courses, and more were being
planned.* Although Ruskin--like these universities and

---

*Based on surveys of labor studies credit and degree programs
by the University and College Labor Education Association, Lois Gray noted that a survey in 1972 turned up
seven degree programs; in 1973, twenty; in 1975, forty-nine
"credit certificate and degree programs" in forty-three

colleges—is supported mainly by public funds, it is, for the most part, self-determining. Virtually all American schools that offer labor studies are part of larger educational organizations and consequently far less independent in making decisions about financial arrangements and educational policies. It should be emphasized that these programs are not offered in the context of a long-term residential school for organized workers and that most of their students are working adults and attend classes part time. The reader should be aware, therefore, that these differences place an important limitation in comparing them with Ruskin.

The absence of systematic analysis of most of the labor colleges, past and present, in the United States also presents some difficulties. There are, however, studies of several existing commuter programs and of Brookwood Labor College, a residential college for workers that was in operation from 1921 to 1937. These studies and my experience in the commuter programs furnish some basis for comparison with Ruskin.

The three commuter programs are located in New York City. These are the Center for Labor Studies, (a division of Empire State College (ESC); the ILR Credit and Certificate Program; and the Labor-Liberal Arts Program.* The last two are segments of the Extension

---

institutions. The surveys did not include noncredit certificate programs or credit programs that offered only a minor in labor studies. In her article (Labor Studies Journal 1 [May 1976]: 36), Gray wrote: "Labor studies constitutes a major toward the associate degree in twenty-eight colleges and universities [twenty-two of them were in community colleges], the bachelor's degree in nine, and a graduate degree in three. In addition, eight institutions offer long-term labor studies certificate courses for college credit that can be applied toward a degree."

*The section describing these commuter programs is a slightly modified version of a description I wrote as part of a larger study: "Labor College and Its Students," Labor Studies Journal 1 (Winter 1977):253-55.

Division of the New York State School of Industrial and Labor Relations, Cornell University, and award certificates to their graduates.* The Center for Labor Studies, as a division of Empire State College, awards associate and bachelor's degrees. It contributes to the support of the ILR Credit and Certificate Program and recognizes the credits earned by students of that program—as do some other colleges. The Center also recognizes the eighteen credits earned by graduates of the Labor-Liberal Arts Program.

For background, it should be noted that Empire State College is an accredited liberal arts college of the State University of New York. It was founded to serve those adults who have not had a college education and whose educational needs are not being met by other colleges. Unlike traditional colleges, it offers individualized learning under a mentor to whom the student is assigned for guidance. A major inducement to adults to enter Empire State College is the credit given by the school for prior learning, including nonacademic work and life experience, as well as previous academic credit. Although union students have welcomed credit for life and work experience, most have rejected the individualized training. In 1971, they persuaded Empire State College to introduce the traditional classroom approach, a procedure that is now followed only in Empire State College's Center for Labor Studies.

Over 280 students have received their associate or bachelor's degree from the Center, more than 80 have received Certificates of Industrial and Labor Relations from the Credit and Certificate Program, and about 550 have received the Certificate in Labor Studies for completion of the Labor-Liberal Arts Program.

---

*Cornell also cooperates in the degree programs of colleges other than Empire State in the State University of New York (SUNY) system: Albany, Brockport, Buffalo, Farmingdale; and with Westchester City College. These programs are similar to the Labor-Liberal Arts Program and are known as Labor Studies. See Ken Gagala, "A Report of the Labor Studies and Management Studies Programs for the Period September 1974 to June 1977," mimeographed (Ithaca: NYSSILR, Cornell University, Division of Extension and Public Service, 1978).

The Labor-Liberal Arts Program introduces the union student to college work by starting with the simplest and most interesting industrial and labor relations subjects and progressing to the most difficult. Along with this set of courses are writing and other study skills courses that are designed to help adults who left school at an early age cope with the more difficult educational subjects associated with the program.

The Center concentrates on labor studies, liberal arts, and other subjects required for a degree. A total of 128 credits or their equivalent are required for a degree, and a minimum of 24 credits must be earned after enrollment in Empire State before a bachelor's degree is awarded.

The Credit and Certificate Program is designed to prepare students for professional careers in industrial and labor relations. On completion of this program a student is awarded a certificate. In the following discussion the Center for Labor Studies and the Credit and Certificate Program will be treated as an integrated whole and called "Labor College."* The Cornell Labor-Liberal Arts Program will be treated separately.

Of all the labor colleges that have existed or now exist in the United States, Brookwood Labor College (1921-37) most closely resembled Ruskin. It was a long-term residential labor college; it was launched by "outsiders"--intellectuals and reformers assisted by leaders of the mineworkers, textile workers, and others whose political beliefs and interest in workers' education roughly resembled that of their counterparts who supported Ruskin in its first decade. Brookwood was one of three residential labor colleges in the United States and, like Ruskin, in its first years was financed mainly by private sources outside the labor movement.[11] Brookwood shared with Ruskin at least one tutor, Charles A. Beard, who taught for both schools. Both Brookwood and Ruskin had distinguished tutors teaching full or part time: R. H. Tawney and G. D. H. Cole, for example, taught at Ruskin and A. J. Muste and David Saposs taught at Brookwood. Both schools had distinguished guest lecturers including Clement Attlee and Lincoln Steffins at Ruskin and Norman

---

*It should be noted that sometimes, in popular use, the term "Labor College" refers to the cooperative effort of all three New York City commuter programs.

Thomas and Sumner Slichter at Brookwood. Both schools had graduates who became distinguished figures.

Each school was founded under different auspices and different circumstances. The Labor-Liberal Arts Program was established by the Extension Division of the New York State School of Industrial and Labor Relations of Cornell University to offer active unionists a liberal education along with union courses.

Prior to the establishment of the Labor-Liberal Arts Program, many of its graduates had attended six-session courses such as shop steward training, principles of grievance procedure, and labor history. Each of the graduates had received a certificate of attendance for each of the courses in which he or she had participated. Their reaction to receiving yet another certificate was, as one student put it, "I have enough certificates to plaster my basement...what I want is the right to receive academic credit and an associate degree." The graduates, many of whom were local union leaders, initiated a campaign to gain the support of the New York City labor movement, especially of Harry Van Arsdale, president of the AFL-CIO New York City Central Labor Council, and called upon the New York State School of Industrial and Labor Relations (ILR) to offer an associate degree in New York City.

The reaction of the ILR faculty members was mixed. Many questioned the ability of the graduates of the Labor-Liberal Arts Program to meet the standards of the school. There were also such problems as who would pay the expenses incurred in founding and conducting an associate degree program in industrial and labor relations in New York City and how New York City colleges would react to yet another associate degree program to be offered in New York City. A committee was appointed by the faculty to study the implications for the school of establishing an associate degree in New York City. After several months, the committee recommended to the faculty that the school offer such a degree and the faculty endorsed the recommendation.

By this time, however, union leaders had persuaded Nelson Rockefeller, then governor of New York State, of the value of the program proposed by the graduates of the Labor-Liberal Arts Program. Rockefeller, in turn, convinced the newly founded Empire State College to open a branch in New York City that would offer not only an associate degree but a bachelor's as well. As a result

of the involvement of Empire State College, the ILR
associate degree was dropped and instead the ILR Credit
and Certificate Program was established as a part of
Labor College with financial support to be provided by
Empire State College. The Labor-Liberal Arts Program
was to continue its curriculum and, along with the ILR
Credit and Certificate Program and the Center for Labor
Studies (ESC), was to be housed in a building owned by
Local 3, International Brotherhood of Electrical Workers
Union.

Brookwood, on the other hand, was founded by trade
unionists who were socialists, "progressives," or mili-
tants. The school's major goal was to furnish union
activists with a liberal education "in order to best
serve the labor movement and through it society."[12]
Both Brookwood and Ruskin at their founding were
supported by social reformers and wanted to change
society. The Labor-Liberal Arts Program and Labor
College, however, are segments of state-supported
colleges with no institutionalized commitment to change
society. Many of their teachers and administrators,
however, are committed to social reform.

Values, Aims, and Curricula

In 1927 Brookwood described its purpose in the
following statement:

> Save for the fact that it stands for
> a new and better order, motivated by
> social values rather than pecuniary
> ones, Brookwood is not a propagandist
> institution. It seeks the truth, free
> from dogma and doctrinaire teaching.
> It believes that the labor and farmer
> movements constitute the most vital
> concrete force working for human free-
> dom, and that by exerting a wise social
> control they can bring in a new era of
> justice and human brotherhood....It is,
> then, a school to educate workers to
> work in the workers' movement. It
> frankly aims not to educate workers out
> of their class.[13]

73

These values and purposes were shared by Ruskin in its first decade and by the Central Labour College during its brief existence. For example, one of Ruskin's founders, Vrooman, said:

> Ruskin Hall, Oxford, although not offi-
> cially connected with the University has
> been founded so as to bring some of the
> exceptional advantages of Oxford within
> reach of workingmen. But it is not intended
> that a man should rise out of his class to
> swell the already crowded professional
> classes. The hope of the institution is
> that each man, by rousing himself, may
> help to raise through influence or precept
> the whole class to which he belongs.[14]

The values and aims of the Central Labour College (later called Labour College) were expressed at the time it was launched by the Plebs League which, as noted earlier, played the key role in its founding. The following is quoted by Craik:

> The second day of August will witness
> the Declaration of Working-Class Inde-
> pendence in Education, a declaration
> which will express the fact that the
> workers prefer to think for themselves
> outside the "indescribable glamour" of
> University life, free from the spell of
> a servile tradition and a slave phil-
> osophy, and to look at the facts as they
> see them from their own standpoint. Our
> answer to those who would swing the re-
> actionary rod over the mental life of
> the working class is only this: we
> neither want your crumbs nor your con-
> descension, your guidance nor your
> glamour, your tuition nor your tradi-
> tion. We have our own historical way
> to follow, our own salvation to achieve,
> and by this sign shall we conquer.[15]

Contemporary labor colleges or their equivalent would probably not subscribe to these statements, although some of their staff and faculty would. On the other hand, all

of the contemporary colleges or their equivalents would
probably agree with the following from the "Joint Statement on Effective Cooperation between Organized Labor
and Higher Education":

> It [cooperation] must be based upon a
> recognition by the educational community
> that labor organizations and collective
> bargaining play a vital and constructive
> role in a modern democratic society.
> Such a cooperative relationship further
> requires that educators fully understand
> the principles and methods of labor edu-
> cation, and that labor organizations
> recognize the need of educational insti-
> tutions to maintain objectivity, intel-
> lectual integrity, academic freedom and
> accepted standards of teaching and
> research.[16]

A fair number of Ruskin's faculty and the staff members
of the two commuter colleges would argue that the statement
does not refer to the need for changing or modifying the
social order as earlier labor colleges have contended.
Nevertheless, Ruskin College today in terms of aims is much
closer to contemporary American labor colleges than to
Ruskin College in its first decade.

While Ruskin has mixed views as to whether its graduates should return to their former activities or go on to
schools of higher education and professional jobs, it
appears to have aims similar to the three American schools,
which have varied in their emphasis on liberal and vocational training. All of them have offered a balanced program that can be used for both a liberal education and
advancing a union career. For example, Labor College
offers four different degrees—A.A., B.A., B.S., and B.P.—
and Brookwood offered a social science curriculum but with
a clear emphasis on courses devoted to the following objectives:

> Men and women who desire to be effective
> and useful in the labor and farmer move-
> ments, whether as rank-and-file members
> or as officials, need in the first place
> a point of view, a method of approach to
> their problem—respect for facts,

> willingness to face facts, ability
> to dig out relevant facts, to solve
> problems, and to make generalizations
> on the basis of facts....They need a
> certain amount of instruction in the
> technique of labor union administration
> and of activities such as speaking, writ-
> ing, organizing, and teaching, in which
> they may be called upon to engage.[17]

Brookwood's curriculum for the first year included
English language, history of civilization, how to study,
psychology, and social economics. In the second year,
it offered union administration, organizing, sociology,
and workers' education. Brookwood did not have the legal
right to offer credits toward a college degree that was
recognized by accredited schools or accrediting institutions. In contrast, the Labor-Liberal Arts Program and
Labor College, as parts of accredited schools, can offer
credit toward such a degree.

The program structures of the schools are also different. Brookwood offered a two-year residential program
that was divided into two four-month semesters a year and
Ruskin has a two-year residential program consisting of
six terms of ten weeks each. The Labor-Liberal Arts Program sponsors a trimester program of twelve weeks each
over a two-year period. Labor College also has a trimester program of twelve weeks each, but because of credit
for life experience it is difficult to estimate how many
years each student spends in the program.

The students at Brookwood carried a full load of
courses as students do at Ruskin. The Labor-Liberal Arts
students attend classes in two subjects once a week for
one and a half hours each. About 80 percent of Labor
College students, however, study the same subject once
a week for three hours over a twelve-week trimester. Although it is permissible to enroll for as many as four
courses a trimester, only a few students have done so.

Worker-Students: Their Motivation and Other Characteristics

The worker-student has been or is motivated to enter
a labor studies program by a desire for self-development and
career development in his or her union. In a study of Labor
College, its students were asked to rank ten reasons why

76

they decided to enroll in the school. Their three
highest choices were "convenience and cost," "a
desire to obtain a college degree for its own sake,"
and "a need to further intellectual or self-development." Ranked seventh was "the college is a labor
college." Students showed similar motives when asked
their reasons for enrolling in the Labor-Liberal Arts
Program. Larry R. Matlack and Charles L. Wright, in
their study of Labor-Liberal Arts, noted that "virtually all students reported enrolling because they
wanted to learn more about the labor movement and
labor problems or because they want to do a better job
in their unions." Only about 5 percent gave such
reasons as wanting a promotion or a better job.
Morris's analysis of the aims of Brookwood indicates
that its students entered to be "equipped...for better
union service."[18] British students entering Ruskin at
different periods may have enrolled in the college to
get a better job, to serve the labor movement more
effectively, or to grow intellectually and be able to
agitate more ably for a new society--or perhaps for
all three reasons.

Despite the differences in the social character
of the eras in which the union activists enrolled in
the four colleges, their motivations for doing so have
been similar. Although there are and have been some
important differences in the recruitment policies of
the four schools, the source of students remains the
same.

Labor College and Labor-Liberal Arts are open-
enrollment schools and accept all applicants. Brookwood accepted those applicants who worked in industry
and held membership in a union for at least one year.
Later it also accepted unorganized workers. The
applicant had to furnish three references, two of them
had to be from "responsible trade unions [sic] able to
vouch for his loyalty to organized labor." Brookwood
did not require any previous educational background,
but placed every new student on probation until ability
to cope with the academic demands of the school was
demonstrated.[19] Ruskin has given preference to early
leavers of school, but within that framework has scru-
tinized the applicants fairly closely before accepting
them. Brookwood, like Ruskin, had a large number of
applicants and used its selections policies to screen
out those they did not believe would be able to meet

their academic responsibilities. Brookwood also had to rely primarily on unions to recruit students.

The Labor-Liberal Arts Program--and Labor College to a much lesser extent--has had to carry on intensive promotional efforts to recruit students who live within commuting distance of the schools. Both have received support from some of the same unions that supported Brookwood; for example, the International Ladies Garment Workers Union, International Brotherhood of Electrical Workers, American Federation of Teachers, and the International Association of Machinists. Some of the newer unions that support the Labor-Liberal Arts Program and the Labor College are District Council 37, American Federation of State, County and Municipal Employees, Communication Workers of America, and the Transport Workers Union. The New York City AFL-CIO Central Labor Council has supported both schools as its predecessor, the New York City AFL Central Labor body, supported Brookwood. Local 3 of the International Brotherhood of Electrical Workers not only pays the tuition fees of its members who satisfactorily complete Labor College courses but assigns its apprentices to attend the school. There are now over one thousand apprentices studying for a Labor College associate degree.

In short, all labor schools have relied heavily on organized labor for students. Ruskin (as did Brookwood) relies on organized workers drawn from similar occupations: miners, machinists (or engineers), railroad workers, textile workers, and others. In addition, Ruskin has and Brookwood had the support of many trades councils. Other organizations that have supported Ruskin and for which there are no American equivalents are cooperative societies, workingmen's clubs, and social clubs of workers.

Whatever the sources of recruits, statistical information about the students who attended the four colleges has been difficult to locate. The writers who have discussed Brookwood, for example, have failed in varying degrees to provide data about the precise social characteristics of the students enrolled each year--including their age, sex, or ethnicity. Similar observations can be made about the data for those who have studied in the other three schools. Table 3 is an attempt to compensate partially for the absence of specific data, systematically arranged on an annual basis, by constructing composite data drawn from various sources.

Table 3: A Comparison of the Four Colleges, According to
Number of Students Enrolled, Percentage of Women,
Blacks, and Other Minorities, Students Working
Full Time and Average Age of Students

School	Enrollment	Women	Blacks & Minorities	Average Age	Working Full Time
Ruskin (1977-78)	168	24%	10-15%	31	5-10%
Labor College (1976-77)	428	33	39	42	85
Labor-Liberal Arts (1973-74)	268	30	41	39	95
Brookwood (1926-27)	40	37[a]	?	26	5-10

Sources: For Labor College, Nash, "Labor College and Its
Student Body," pp. 254-57, and Bill Goode, "Motivational
Orientation of Trade Unionists Who Are Attending Labor College"
(a manuscript submitted as a dissertation for an Ed.D., Rut-
gers University, 1980), table 40, pp. 89-90. For Labor-
Liberal Arts Program, Matlack and Wright, Two Nontraditional
Programs of Higher Education, pp. 29-36. For Ruskin College,
Reports and Accounts for Year Ended 31 July 1978. For Brook-
wood Labor College, Brooks, Clint, p. 85, and Bulletin and
Announcement of Courses, p. 11.

[a]Data about Brookwood female students are drawn from Helen
Norton, "Brookwood in Its First Decade," Labor Age 20, no. 5
(May 1931):19, quoted by Gwen Wells, "Brookwood Labor College,"
mimeographed (Ithaca, N.Y.: student paper, 1979).

The demographic characteristics of the four schools outlined in table 3 show that the Labor-Liberal Arts Program and the Labor College are much larger schools than Ruskin and that their students have far less time to devote to their studies. As a result, these students lack the intensive contact with teachers and co-students that facilitates receptivity to academic values. In addition, Labor-Liberal Arts and Labor College students are older than the Ruskin students and more of them are women and members of minorities. Unfortunately, these characteristics, even today, restrict occupational opportunities.

In concluding this segment on characteristics of students in the different colleges, a number of generalizations may be added. Based on my personal observation of Ruskin students and my experience in teaching Labor College and Labor-Liberal Arts students, I conclude that Ruskin students are probably better able to fit into the student role than the students of the New York commuter colleges. Ruskin students, for example, write and speak more ably. This difference may be in part because English is a second language for 10 to 15 percent of the students enrolled in the Labor-Liberal Arts Program and because more of them have had little formal schooling. Differences can also be attributed in part to the ability of residential schools like Ruskin to draw from a national cross-section of applicants who are more literate and politically sophisticated than many of the students in the Labor College and the Labor-Liberal Arts Program. These attributes, when added to the advantages of studying in a residential school, help the students become more receptive to the academic expectations of the school and achieve higher status jobs in the labor movement and elsewhere.

Student Influence

Because of their political backgrounds and ongoing participation in the Labour party or other working-class parties, Ruskin students are more critical of their tutors and readings. Such participation contributes to the sophistication of the students and to their ability to speak more effectively and to think in more abstract terms than the students whose experience is confined to the union. Frequently the political activists have union experience

because their political views motivated them to become
active in the union movement. Brookwood students
probably had similar attributes since many of them were
active in socialist and other working-class organizations.
Brookwood students, like their teachers, were influenced
by what they perceived to be new opportunities for social
change as a result of the Russian revolution and by the
possibilities of "organizing the unorganized," especially
the unskilled whom the AFL had failed to reach. Unions
such as the International Ladies Garment Workers Union
and the United Mine Workers, both of which had socialists
in their leadership, sent promising workers to Brookwood
and contributed to their support. The student body con-
sisted mainly of "left" students including "a not insignificant number of communists."[20] The Labor-Liberal Arts
students and those who founded Labor College were influenced by the struggles of women and blacks for credentials
and by labor leaders who believed that education of their
members would aid the union. Very few Labor College or
Labor-Liberal Arts students were or are radical or socialist. The issues of the 1970s, unlike those of the 1900s
and the 1920s, were not crucial or persuasive enough to
rally labor college teachers and students. Unlike the
students of Ruskin and Brookwood, the Labor-Liberal Arts
and Labor College students are politically to the right
of their teachers.

The success of the students in founding Labor College,
however, illustrates how active and influential they have
been in the school. Labor College students also persuaded
the school administration to eliminate the two-semester
academic year and replace it with a trimester year. In
fact, it appears that labor students in the United States
and Great Britain have generally played a more influential
role in their schools than most conventional students.

Brookwood had a student association that exercised an
advisory role in educational areas and in student discipline
and activities. The faculty and students each had a standing committee, and these committees met jointly to discuss
school problems.[21] More recently, the student associations
of other labor schools have tended to treat administrators
and teachers as adversaries and to act as grievance committees. They negotiate with college authorities on such
issues as methods of evaluating students, administrative
delays, curriculum, and related matters. The student
associations are usually effective in this role because
many administrators and faculty do not resist reasonable

81

demands. Teachers and tutors are sympathetic to unions and to democratic and collective efforts to reform the social order. They have a special affection for working-class adults and their goals. In brief, the redemptive view of students by teachers and tutors, their perspectives, and their background prompt them--despite the problems--to cooperate with union students and their associations.

Effect of Labor Education on the Students

I have discussed at some length the effect or Ruskin on its students. And, although not enough time has elapsed to make a definitive judgment, tentatively it may be said that the Labor-Liberal Arts Program has not had the same effect on its students, especially if measured by their accomplishments after receiving their certificates. If, however, we consider the limited amount of time that fully employed students can devote to their studies, the number of years that they, especially the older ones, have been away from school, and their average age (39), the significance of the Labor-Liberal Arts Program for the students takes on more importance.

Support for this conclusion is found in the study of the Labor-Liberal Arts Program by Matlack and Wright. They noted that "unquestionably, the most universal impact experienced by [Labor-Liberal Arts] students...was the improvement of their self images." They have "greater poise in meeting people, greater confidence in doing their jobs and a greater sense of self-worth and self-esteem." As a Cornell staff member observed, "It was as if they had become new people." Matlack and Wright explained these changes in the students' personalities by pointing out that they were for the first time successful where previously they had failed. The praise and congratulations of family, friends, and coworkers at the graduation ceremonies, the writers suggested, were in large measure responsible for their increased self-confidence. Matlack and Wright have two reservations about the changes in the students. They noted that although the school affected the students' educational aspirations and union activity, it "had little impact on the social dimensions of their lives." They questioned "whether the other effects are cosmetic or real in terms of improved basic skills.... Given the nature of these...programs, significant upgrading of basic educational skills is not likely."[22]

Although there are no large-scale studies of how the Labor College has affected the attitudes of its graduates, a brief study of forty-six graduates found that as a result of attending the school (1) 59 percent reported that their perceptions of work had changed; (2) 55 percent now viewed labor unions from "an altered perspective"; (3) 52 percent "believed that their perspective on management had changed"; and (4) 50 percent indicated that their experience at Labor College "had kindled an interest in academic study or, more specifically, in the study of industrial and labor relations."[23]

GENERAL OBSERVATIONS

Like Ruskin and Brookwood, Labor College and the Labor-Liberal Arts Program are pioneer schools that share a number of characteristics: a curriculum featuring labor studies and social sciences, teachers and students with union backgrounds, graduates who move up the union ladder or--with the exception of Brookwood-- go on to schools of higher education. Labor College and the Labor-Liberal Arts Program also have problems similar to those Brookwood had and Ruskin still has in educating their students. The working-class student apparently deals more easily with the concrete, specific, and practical than with the abstract, general, and theoretical, and consequently requires assistance in overcoming this difficulty.[24]

All four programs have received support from the union movement and all but Brookwood have been the beneficiaries of financial support from governmental agencies.

Ruskin has been close to the TUC--Great Britain's national federation of labor--and the commuter colleges have been close to the New York City Central Labor Council and its affiliates. Ruskin has followed an independent academic path, and the TUC and most of its affiliates have acknowledged Ruskin's academic integrity and competence. Brookwood, however, in the tradition established by the Central Labour College, politicized academic roles by becoming what Morris referred to as "a center of trade union opposition" to those unions and leaders it considered conservative. As a consequence, its main targets were leaders of the AFL.[25] According to Muste, Brookwood initially stressed the "factual approach," for example, educating its students to base their arguments on empirical evidence and emphasizing "how to think" rather than "what to think."[26] Later, Brookwood stressed "what to think," as the school became more involved in advocating industrial unionism and criticizing the AFL. As a result, Brookwood, like Central Labour College, lost financial and other support from the mainstream of the labor movement.

The other three colleges have been able to maintain a friendly relationship with the labor movement through mutual consultation. Participation by union officials on the advisory board and allocation of student scholarships by unions have buttressed the relationship, and as a result these schools have survived.

VIII.

The Challenge to Labor and Adult Education

RESIDENTIAL VS. COMMUTER PROGRAMS

Many of the differences between Ruskin on the one hand and such commuter programs as Labor College and the Labor-Liberal Arts Program on the other are related to the advantages of residential facilities that provide the isolation and segregation needed to acquire new values and new norms. Isolation from one's friends and family makes it easier to modify old attitudes and to form new friendships. Residential conditions also speed up integration among the students and between the students and tutors. In turn, this increased interaction, as discussed by George Homans, tends to strengthen shared sentiments and values. The residential college also provides more extracurricular activities than does the commuter college. Amitai Etzioni found that a school, by extending the scope of its activities, increases the "involvement of the student in the school and the school's influence over him." Another writer, J. F. C. Harrison, in referring to Ruskin noted that the residential college leaves a deeper impression than just the "acquisition of knowledge."[1]

Compared to a commuter college a residential college provides a better atmosphere for learning: it allows more time for study, permits more detachment, reduces pressures associated with home and family, and extends opportunities for discussions with tutors. Consequently, students can enroll in more courses, do more research, write more papers, and do more assignments. Thus, the student at a residential school is more conscious of his or her student role because it is a major activity. Occupying a new role enables the new student to view old associates and groups and their patterns of behavior from a new perspective. In addition, in the long-term residential college, there are

more full-time teachers who have the leisure time to
write for publication and to prepare for their classes.
They have also had more opportunities to accumulate
experience and develop ongoing relationships with students. One important reason for the superiority of
residential colleges is that the ratio of ad hoc teachers
to full-time teachers is much lower in the residential
than in the nonresidential college.

Another difference between Ruskin and the commuter
colleges is that Ruskin is more demanding of its students
in required reading, homework, and its method of evaluating students. These expectations are more feasible, at
least in part, in the residential setting for full-time
students than in the commuter setting for part-time students with full-time jobs. In addition, the tutorial
system requires a student to be more enterprising and more
independent in meeting academic responsibilities. The
tutored student receives more individual guidance and
criticism of his or her work than the student in the conventional classroom.

Other advantages of the tutorial method are that it
permits greater adjustment to the student's needs and
preferences and the development of the student does not
have to depend on the pace of other students. Thus, the
education is deeper and broader with more room for student initiative. At the same time, criticism delivered
in private meetings is more easily accepted by the student, and the student can ask more questions and follow
through on a particular strand of thought. A major problem, however, is that students who are not self-starters
find it more difficult to adjust to tutorials than to
classroom teaching. This type of student also frequently
needs the support of peers to help cope with the tensions
and problems associated with returning to school as a
mature but educationally undernourished student.

Mentoring--roughly equivalent to tutoring--is available to Labor College students but more than 90 percent
of them have rejected it in favor of traditional classroom
teaching. If more students chose the mentoring method,
longer hours for both student and mentor would be required
and more students would have to do their academic work during the day. Thus, financial aid for students would have
to be increased and more mentors would have to be employed.
It is doubtful that the two commuter schools could afford
mentoring as it is practiced in Ruskin.

CONFLICT, IDEOLOGY, AND PROBLEMS

Despite its advantages, residential education does not preclude conflict between the schools and the students. A focus on Ruskin illustrates, however, that the discord between adult and labor residential colleges and their students is occasional and limited.

Ruskin has had periodic clashes--punctuated by long intervals of peace--between school authorities and students. The clash of interests in Ruskin is affected by its struc- ture as a residential school, including its function as a "hotel," and by the desire of students to participate in its government. The residential college is apt to find students complaining, for instance, about the cost of room and board and the rules regulating hotel life (for example, the requirement that students keep their rooms clean and tidy). Differences in this area with administrators stim- ulate the interest of the student in participating in the government of the school.

Differences between the school and the students, for example, may be also sharpened and elaborated because the students in a residential college interact more frequently than do those in a commuter college. As a result, they share their information and insight about problems in the school. This is especially true of Ruskin students whose common background as members of unions and working-class parties increases their ability to challenge the school administration and gives them a sense of legitimacy in doing so.

Although the Ruskin students have won the right to participate in decision making at the school, they con- tinue to try to influence decisions over methods of assess- ment, the cost of room and board, and other areas that re- late to their role as students. A perennial dispute be- tween the administrators and the students has been over the students' role in the government of the school and in determining its purposes and direction. Nevertheless, serious conflict between students and school officials is episodic and infrequent as is demonstrated by the fact that over a period of eighty years only three major clashes took place.*

---

*One exception to this claim is Fircroft College which was closed from 1975 to 1980 because of differences between tutors and students on the one hand and the governors of the school and the principal on the other. Some of the issues in dispute

Ideology, often expressed as dogma, reinforces the difference between the school officialdom and the students. The difference is expressed in the charge by students that "impartial" education is propaganda in disguise. For example, Ruskin students have persistently complained about the content of teaching and tutorials. G. D. H. Cole and Raymond Postgate noted that Ruskin students in 1908 protested that "the character of the teaching...was merely a disguised propaganda in favour of the capitalist system," a complaint still heard at Ruskin.[2] The other side of the coin is the comment of Robert Peel who characterized teaching at Central Labour College and NCLC as "a strait jacket of propagandist ideas in the guise of education." Many of the students would agree with Gaetano Salvemini who in another context said that "impartiality is either a delusion of the simple-minded, or a banner of the opportunist and the dishonest." In the American equivalent of labor colleges, the debate is among the labor educators around a similar issue: should the teacher encourage students to make up their own minds after a full and impartial presentation of the issues or should the teacher promote the values of the labor movement?

Ideology also plays a part in the running debates students have with each other and with their tutors. Though ideology may add more purpose and meaning to the life of the student, constant debates and polemics may have a negative effect in the sense that the arguments may distract students from their academic responsibilities. For example, R. D. Sealey writes that

> Within Ruskin there are many social groups based on political affiliations which are competing for leadership of the student body. This results in an almost continuous state of tension. Outwardly these differences are covered over with the broad generalization of "We are aiming for the same end but in different ways."

were the right to free speech, social relevance of courses, dogma and ideology, and differing conceptions of liberal education and liberal studies.

But this underlying tension distracts
the students from their studies.[3]

Some of the problems may not lead to conflict between
the students and the school, but they often become important
in relation to academic matters. When the tutor, for
example, wants to teach, the students want to preach; when
the tutor tries to individualize instruction by helping
students to learn to think for themselves, the students
strive to act and think as members of an interest group.
According to Dr. V. Treadwell, a tutor interviewed at Ruskin
(September 1978):

> The odd thing about here of course is
> that while we, as tutors, are emphasiz-
> ing the one to one relationship which
> is involved in academic work, students
> in their own organizations are trying
> to re-emphasize the collectivity of
> students.

Other problems for the school that have not been articu-
lated in the literature or discussed formally in interviews
are nevertheless there. Among those problems are maintaining
academic standards, recruiting students who will meet the
standards of the school, employing tutors who have both union
and academic backgrounds, the role of the school as a vocational agency, the school as a symbol of the establishment,
and pressure of the students on the school to adopt a Marxist
or socialist orientation.[4] Many of these problems are built
into the school structure and goals and are also found in
other labor colleges whether or not they are residential
schools.

Behind the debate on more democracy for the student
and other related questions in most labor colleges are
the unspoken assumptions that often reflect opinion about
what a labor college is or should be. At the opening of
a new Ruskin building in 1911, Ben Tillet, general secretary
of the Docker's Union, expressed his hope that the school
would bring about a change in the social order:

> I want to see this College teach its
> students what their lives mean under
> the law of their country....I want the
> commonplaces of life to be understood,
> and the difficulties that our social

> system presents to the working classes.
> We talk so much about what the working
> class is, what it ought to be, and what
> should be done to it, but up till now
> we have been rather patronized, and
> the workers of the country love a lord--
> they love the sight of opulence and the
> sight of office and distinction, but I
> am hoping that this College is going to
> kill that form of flunkeyism, at least
> in everyone who comes to it.[5]

More recently, Hammonds, a former Ruskin student, described a labor college as "an agency of change" and charged that Ruskin had compromised that role by becoming a virtual appendage of Oxford University. Others, such as a student quoted by Smith, view Ruskin as little more than "a prep-school for a university," implying that it has abandoned responsibility for training students for roles in the labor movement. (Of the various criticisms made of Ruskin, this one appears to be the most prevalent.) A related criticism of Ruskin, also quoted by Smith, is that it "enjoys the reputation of being a 'labour college' because of its selection procedure not because of its feedback into the movement, although this is not insignificant."[6] Another description of a labor college, in Craik, is that it fights "for liberation from capitalist and political domination." Related to this approach is the characterization of a labor college as one which follows "an independent working-class education" whose core program (e.g., economics, history, and political science) is taught from a Marxist point of view. This approach was offered in the early 1900s and early 1970s and may be called the "political" approach.[7]

Still another description of a labor college, by Cattermole, is that it serves as a "staff college for the labour movement."[8] But, a description of Ruskin College given me by a school official (interview, August 1978) rejects the chracterization of Ruskin as a labor, vocational, or socialist school:

> A significant proportion [of our stu-
> dents] would think of us as a labor
> college or socialist college in the
> ideological sense. And it's a surprise
> when they come here to find that the

curricula program is nonideological,
is objective in the university sense.
A significant number of them would
probably think that we offer an easier
pathway to full-time employment in the
trade union and labor movements than
is in fact the case.

If there does not appear to be a consensus about the
nature of a labor college in Britain, matters are no better
in the United States. Here the debate centers on the nature
of labor studies, the "academization of labor education,"
and the limitations of the industrial and labor relations
curriculum. Disagreements abound about what courses a labor
studies program should comprise, on what discipline or disciplines it should be based, how it should differ from
conventional college industrial and labor relations programs, and whether traditional union role education or
"tool" courses belong in the curriculum.[9]

The disputes in both countries are between those who view
unions as a tool for improving the immediate lot of workers
and those who view them as an organized means for achieving
basic structural changes in society. Changes in the strength,
structure, and goals of the unions shape and stimulate changes
in workers' education and the views of those active in it.

A major problem for leaders of the labor movement in
the United States is that some of the most able and committed union activists who go to labor colleges leave the union
movement. Thus, the labor college becomes a path for social
advancement and for assimilation into managerial ranks.
As Hopper and Osborn said, in their discussion of long-term
residential colleges that offer a liberal education for working-class adults, a majority of the graduates have not returned "to their former jobs as more politically and socially
aware members of the community."[10] This result is contrary
to the hopes of those in labor education.

Other problems of Ruskin and the other labor colleges
relate to the quality of the program, the absence of adequate academic credit for use in schools of higher education
or graduate schools, and the failure of corporations to
give educational leaves to employees who attend residential
schools.

TRENDS

Especially in the last two decades, the growth of adult and continuing education in Great Britain, as well as in the United States, has encouraged many universities to open or expand intramural or extension departments. This growth has also encouraged local educational authorities to open or expand colleges of "further" education and community colleges. These colleges offer courses for union stewards and others in "role education," which includes teaching grievance procedure as well as courses in occupational safety and health.[11]

Another example of growth of adult education in Great Britain is Northern College, sometimes called the Ruskin of the North, which opened in October 1978 and represents a major development in long-term residential education for labor and community activists. Its program and aims go beyond those of Ruskin and the other long-term residential colleges for adults. Its principal, Michael Barratt Brown, has indicated that (1) it will serve students drawn from unions and local and immigrant communities; (2) it will offer short-term courses of five to ten weeks to community leaders and a one-year certificate program as well as a two-year diploma program for those who seek to make a major change in their occupations; (3) it will not demand any tests or other qualifications for admission except a letter indicating why the student seeks to enter the school; (4) it will provide a meeting place and focus for community activities in music, drama, local studies, and research; and (5) it will experiment with different courses and approaches. Some educators believe that Northern College, despite the stated intentions of its supporters, may become a competitor of Ruskin.[12]

Furthermore, the number of trade union training colleges in Great Britain has increased. In addition to the TUC Training College, there are nine unions that sponsor their own residential training colleges.* The

---

*These are the General and Municipal Workers Union; Electrical, Electronic, Telecommunication Union/Plumbing Trades Union; Association of Scientific, Technical and Managerial Staffs; Transport and General Workers' Union; the Civil and Public Services Association; National Association of Schoolmasters; National Union of Railwaymen; National Union of Teachers; and Post Office Engineering Union.

availability of these programs and schools, including
the Open University, and the relative ease with which
workers in Britain can enter them raise the question
of whether or not there is a need for Ruskin or other
residential adult colleges.

H. D. Hughes wrote in the 1979 Ruskin College
report that Ruskin does not see these union-owned
colleges as competitors "but in fact complementary...
to Ruskin courses, concentrating as they do on 'role
education' and training for specific purposes." Indeed
Ruskin considers them a source of students. As for the
competition of colleges of "further education," Ruskin
can point to the opening of Northern College and the re-
opening of Fircroft as indicators of the growing need
for both labor and adult colleges. Furthermore, an
increasing number of universities--about a dozen--
recognize the diplomas of Ruskin and other long-term
residential adult colleges, exempt graduates from some
of the degree requirements, and extend credit for
academic work performed at these colleges.[13]

Some tutors and interested observers believe that,
in view of these new developments, Ruskin standards will
be lowered in order to recruit the desirable number of
students--a few say the process has already begun. Many
of the tutors, graduates, students, and TUC educators
interviewed perceived Ruskin as a second-chance school
or a prep school.[14] Other tutors and former Ruskin
students said that those who enrolled in the current
period are brighter and more sophisticated than those
who preceded them; others expressed an opposite opinion.

CONCLUSION

In retrospect the secession of the students of the
Plebs League to launch another college (CLC) was fortunate
for Ruskin. This split, although not appreciated at the
time, served Ruskin well. It demonstrated that the school
was "responsible" and loyal to the TUC and to other organizations that were among the dominant forces in the labor
movement. Paradoxically, partly because of this close
relationship, Ruskin maintained its academic support and
its access to desirable students. In brief, the events
of 1909 started a train of developments that reinforced
Ruskin's reputation for academic excellence and indirectly
gave students access to jobs with more intellectual challenge,
more status, and more financial rewards.

When the education and accomplishments of Ruskin students are compared with those of other labor college students, the evidence indicates that the former obtained more jobs in the helping professions and played more of a role in the union movement. In addition to these characteristics of the educational process, one might suggest that those accomplishments were due, at least in part, to differences in the students themselves. Ruskin students were more class-conscious and socialist-minded, and were probably better writers and speakers. Although there were some outstanding Brookwood graduates, their accomplishments were not nearly as impressive as those of Ruskin graduates. The contribution of Brookwood was reduced because it never had the real support from leading AFL officials as Ruskin had from TUC leaders. When the AFL withdrew its endorsement of Brookwood, student enrollment declined and by 1937 the school was closed.[15] In addition, one should note that Brookwood's effective life as a school lasted for about twelve years, not long enough to equal the contribution of Ruskin or the CLC.

In the United States, there was no enduring equivalent to Ruskin. Perhaps a major reason for this was the inability of the American Federation of Labor to make use of speakers, teachers, journalists, writers, and lecturers to "popularize its cause." In addition, Selig Perlman noted that "the profit motive, the climbing impulse, conspicuous leisure, and the 'curse of manual work' are potent influences which have drained both the workers' and farmers' groups of needed talent for leadership."[16] To this list of causes, one might add the inability of AFL leaders to cooperate with socialists, intellectuals, reformers, and women leaders in workers' education in their endeavors to develop labor colleges and other educational organizations in the early decades of the twentieth century.

The current labor leadership, successors to the AFL and the CIO, has a more positive attitude toward labor colleges despite the fact that instructors critical of AFL-CIO officialdom teach in educational programs offered to active unionists. The attitude of the AFL-CIO leadership is partly a consequence of the support given by unions that were founded in the struggle against the policies of the old AFL and wholeheartedly supported labor education and labor colleges.*

---

*I refer, for instance, to the United Auto Workers, the Communication Workers of America, the United Steelworkers Union, and the Oil, Chemical and Atomic Workers Union. A number of former

Support by the British labor movement continues to make it possible for Ruskin to recruit, train, and educate individuals who contribute to the leadership pool at all levels of the labor movement. Ruskin also has been able to maintain an academic climate in which adherents and sympathizers of working-class parties can debate, learn, and intellectually stimulate one another. Moreover, it is fortunate to have been founded when the Labour party, the WEA, the Socialist Labour party, and especially the TUC and its affiliates, and other labor organizations were either being founded or expanded. Finally, the school has been able to maintain a moderate and balanced tone and an able body of tutors to help preserve the long-term residential school.

Ruskin, like other labor and long-term residential adult colleges that have survived, has a commitment to liberal education that increases the ability of individuals to evaluate and take effective joint action about the conditions and character of their lives. Commitment to a liberal education does not preclude its use to help working-class activists legitimate their social values and common goals.

Finally, Ruskin College has been able to maintain a moderate and balanced tone and an able group of tutors to help preserve its character. Compared to the other long-term residential colleges I have discussed, Ruskin gives greater attention to the interplay of tradition and change, of theory and practice, of individualism and collectivism, and of academic values and working-class values.

More specifically, residential schools provide the conditions for the intellectual growth and development of union activists who seek another opportunity to acquire higher education in consonance with their needs as individuals and members of the working class. As the Russell Committee pointed out in its discussion of the contribution made by Ruskin and the other long-term residential colleges for adults,

> Full-time study makes sustained intellectual demands and, when combined with individual tuition and the full life

---

AFL unions, such as the International Association of Machinists and the International Brotherhood of Electrical Workers, also became supporters of labor education.

95

> of the college, produces much more
> rapid intellectual growth than is
> possible under conditions of part-time
> study. None of this would be within
> the reach of, for example, students
> from deprived backgrounds without the
> change of environment and the temporary
> release from voluntary activities and
> family responsibilities that a residen-
> tial course offers.[17]

The one-week summer schools which unions hold in cooperation with universities have shown American and British labor educators and union leaders the advantages of residential college education. These one-week schools have stimulated intellectual growth, a clearer understanding of the union movement, a broader social perspective, and stronger fraternal bonds among the participants. This study of Ruskin College indicates what can be accomplished when the possibilities of long-term residential workers' education are more fully realized.

Appendixes

APPENDIX A

RUSKIN COLLEGE, OXFORD
PARTICULARS OF SCHOLARSHIPS AND ADMISSION
1978-79*

I. RUSKIN COLLEGE

The college is open to men and women between the ages of 20 and 40, and candidates are selected on the basis of their general record, and an essay, followed by a personal interview. No formal educational qualifications are required.

College fees and charges are prescribed by the Department of Education and Science and are subject to annual review....

[See "welcoming letter" for 1978/79 fees.]

The year consists of three terms: 9 October to 15 December 1978; 15 January to 29 March; 23 April to 4 July 1979.

Details of courses are contained in the College Prospectus, which is available on application to the College.

II. SCHOLARSHIPS AND ADMISSION TO THE COLLEGE

Candidates with three years' residential qualification in the United Kingdom are eligible for Adult Education State Bursaries on the national scales covering "approved fees," maintenance and dependants' allowances, etc. Trade Union

---

*Information is excerpted from Ruskin College form RC/SCH/78.

and other scholarships and awards described in this leaflet
are normally of a value of up to 215 pounds for the academic
year and are supplementary to basic awards made under the
Adult Education State Bursary Scheme.

Candidates for scholarships and those seeking admission
to the College (except where otherwise indicated below) are
asked to complete the application form RC/APP/1 in duplicate,
and submit it to Ruskin College, Oxford, by 1 March 1978
with an essay of between 1,000 and 2,000 words on ONE of
the following subjects:

1. "The goals of full employment, economic growth
and stable prices." What policies are required
to achieve these?

2. Do we have to make a choice between a more
equal, just, and compassionate society and one
with greater economic efficiency?

3. Outline the wage and salary structure at
your place of work. What difficulties are
likely to arise in the return to free collective bargaining?

4. Are there circumstances in which violence
is justifiable for political ends?

5. Draw upon your own experience of life in
discussing what contribution autobiography
can make to the study of history.

6. "The novel has been a source of great
pleasure." Should this be so, and in
what ways? Make detailed reference to
at least two novels that you have read.

7. What are the main influences determining the division of labour between men
and women in society.

8. (Applied Social Studies candidates).
How does a situation of high unemployment
amongst young people affect the social
workers' role?

Essays set for TUC Educational Trust scholarships
may be submitted as an alternative to one of the above,
for College admission and scholarships.

Candidates are also requested to submit a brief
autobiographical note indicating (i) the main experiences which have induced them to apply to Ruskin,
(ii) their objectives in the future, and (iii) the
part they expect a College course to play in attain-
ing those objectives.

III. GENERAL SCHOLARSHIPS

A. The Robert Addy Hopkinson Educational Trust offers
up to THREE scholarships, open to men and women between
the ages of 20 and 40....

B. Ruskin College offers TWO scholarships open to
immigrants who have been in this country for at least
three years, and who are eligible for consideration
for Adult Education State Bursaries....

C. The AUEW (TASS) and the Ruskin Fellowship jointly
offer a DAVID KITSON bursary to students with experience of trade unionism or political movements in
Africa. Candidates may be asked to submit an essay
on a topic related to African affairs. Enquiries
to General Secretary, Ruskin College, Oxford.

Applicants for the awards described in this
section will also be considered for any Trade Union
Appeal Fund Scholarships...for which they may be eligible.

IV. TRADE UNION APPEAL AND FUND SCHOLARSHIPS AND BURSARIES

(A) Trade Union Appeal Fund Scholarships
The Ferdie Smith Scholarship and TWO other awards
are open to members of the following unions: [Fifty-
six unions are listed under this heading.]

(B) General Federation of Trade Unions (Hodgson
Scholarship)
The Hodgson Scholarship is open to members of
unions affiliated to the G.T.F.U....

(C) Individual Trade Union Scholarships
The following scholarships/bursaries are offered to
their members by individual trade unions. Successful
applicants eligible also for major awards under the Adult
Education State Bursary scheme (see Section II) will
receive supplementary awards up to the prescribed limit.
Rural Workers: Open to members of the National
Union of Agricultural and Allied Workers....
A.U.E.W. Workers: (a) Engineering Section--ONE or
more awards are offered to members of the Amalgamated
Union of Engineering Workers (Engineering Section)....
(b) Technical, Administrative and Supervisory Section--
the DAVID KITSON scholarship is open to members of
A.U.E.W. (Technical, Administrative and Supervisory
Section)....
Civil and Public Services Staff: The L. C. WHITE
MEMORIAL SCHOLARSHIP is open to members of the Civil
and Public Services Association....
Coalminers: Up to FOUR awards are open to members
of the N.U.M. under the ROBERT SMILLIE MEMORIAL SCHOLAR-
SHIP scheme endowed by the National Union of Mineworkers.
Awards are also available under a FOUNDRESS SCHOLARSHIP
scheme which is open to all miners.
General and Municipal Workers: The General and
Municipal Workers' Union offer (a) the COLIN CHIVERS
MEMORIAL SCHOLARSHIP open to members who have previously
attended either of the Union's Residential Colleges;
(b) Up to THREE other awards open to G.M.W.U. members
generally....
Graphical Workers: Up to THREE awards are offered
to members of the National Graphical Association....
TWO awards are offered to members of the Society of
Graphical and Allied Trades....
Inland Revenue Staff: ONE or more awards are open
to members of the Inland Revenue Staff Federation....
Journalists: Up to TWO awards are offered to
members of the National Union of Journalists.
Post Office Engineers: The CHARLES HOWARD SMITH
SCHOLARSHIP is open to members of the Post Office
Engineering Union....
Public Employees: The National Union of Public
Employees has given a sum to provide up to THREE BRYN
ROBERTS Bursaries. Members of unions in the public
services, including central government, local govern-
ment, education and hospital services are eligible....

Seamen: ONE or more awards are open to members of the National Union of Seamen....

Distributive and Allied Trades: Awards are available under the SIR JOSEPH HALLSWORTH and the SIR ALAN BIRCH scholarship schemes to members of the Union of Shop, Distributive and Allied Workers....

Tailors and Garment Workers: The ANDREW CONLEY MEMORIAL SCHOLARSHIP is open to members of the National Union of Tailors and Garment Workers....

Transport and General Workers: Bursaries are available to members of the Transport and General Workers' Union with not less than two years' financial membership....

Construction Workers: ONE award is offered under the UCATT CENTENARY SCHOLARSHIP scheme to members of the Union of Construction and Allied Trades and Technicians....

Professional, Clerical and Computer Staff: The Association of Professional, Executive, Clerical and Computer Staff (APEX) offers up to SEVEN bursary awards to members attending Ruskin or one of the other adult residential colleges or the L.S.E. Trade Union Studies Course....

V. OTHER SCHOLARSHIPS

Trades Union Congress Educational Trust

The Trades Union Congress Educational Trust offer FIVE one-year awards open to members of unions affiliated to the T.U.C.... Candidates for T.U.C.E.T. awards who wish to be considered for other scholarships listed should make separate application to the College in accordance with Section II.

VI. INTERVIEWS

Interviews for these scholarships and for admission will be held in April, May or June, and candidates placed on short-lists will be notified accordingly.

VII. DIPLOMA IN APPLIED SOCIAL STUDIES

(Recognised by Central Council for Education and Training in Social Work)

Students accepted for this course will be eligible for grants from their L.E.A.'s unless they are seconded by their employing body in the field of social work. Adult Education State Bursaries are <u>not</u> available in respect of this "professional" course.

Candidates for the course should contact the Course Tutor (Applied Social Studies), Ruskin Hall, Headington, Oxford (phone 63894). Formal application is through a central Clearing House system; candidates will be required to submit an essay (see Section II) on the topic "How does a situation of high unemployment amongst young people affect the social workers' role?" Closing date: 1 March 1978.

C. HOPLEY,

General Secretary

APPENDIX B

RUSKIN COLLEGE
TWO YEAR DIPLOMA COURSE IN
LABOUR STUDIES
Autumn 1975

This is a two-year course in social studies whose
central theme is the study of labour.

1. Compulsory Subjects
    A special feature of the Labour Studies course is to
ensure that students who complete it are able to link analytical and conceptual study with empirical enquiry and
practical application. It is for this reason that the
course requires students to reach at least an adequate
level of attainment in two fields that are necessary
instruments both for the effectiveness of further study
and for independent student research work. These two
subjects are English Expression and Statistics.
    Students are also required to study Industrial
Relations, a subject which cuts across and borrows from
a number of separate academic disciplines. Classes and
lectures on this subject (under various headings: 'Trade
Union Government'; 'Labour Economics'; 'Industrial
Relations', for example) extend through the course.

2. Research Project
    All students are required to undertake an approved
research project testing ability to organise and analyse
relatively complex material. The tutorial supervision
of the project is normally in the fifth term. The thesis

103

in its completed form is submitted (two copies) at the
beginning of the sixth term. It is assessed by both an
internal tutor and an external examiner; assessment
includes oral examination.

The educational value of a major project, carried
through with tutorial supervision, is very considerable.
It enables students to discover what level of work they
can achieve when they move beyond the relatively restricted
range of normal tutorial assignments. It enables genuine
originality of work. It gives valuable training in the
management of independent research work, and in the hand-
ling of original material and analysis. In many cases it
enables a student to grasp in practice the relationship
between aspects of a problem that have previously been
studied as separate disciplines. (A separate paper 'Notes
for Guidance on College Theses' is available for each student, and should be carefully studied.)

3. Tutorials

The main method of teaching at the College is through
tutorials. Normally a student chooses a particular subject
a term; he is allocated to a tutor who is responsible for
his work in that subject during the term. The twelve options available, of which a student has to study four, are
listed below in Section 4. Each student is free to choose
his subjects, but within certain limits. It is not desirable to concentrate narrowly and exclusively on a single
specialist subject to the exclusion of other social science
disciplines. The approach that has been adopted is that a
disciplined approach to labour institutions and needs
requires a broad appreciation of relevant 'humanities' and
the ability to work at a relatively advanced level both
within a specialism and by combining different specialisms.

There are six terms in the two year course. Students
study four subjects for a term each through weekly tutorials.
One of these subjects may be taken as a MAJOR requiring at
least one-and-a-half terms' tutorial work, and appropriate
classes as recommended by the tutor or adviser. Alternatively, the four subjects can be studied tutorially for one
term each, and extra tutorial time be taken in one of the
compulsory subjects (English, Statistics or Industrial
Relations). Or a fifth subject, unconnected with the twelve
listed options, may be studied. Performance in tutorial
subjects is assessed both by tutorial reports and by examination.

The regulations do not identify in detail the curriculum content of the tutorial subjects. The subjects specified simply indicate a particular subject area. Thus it is normal for a student and tutor to discuss each term the areas of the subject to be covered, and there is an opportunity for students to pursue any special interest and needs. There is, however, a general requirement covering all tutorial subjects, that a term's tutorials should cover the analytical concepts and main empirical material of the particular subject. It is the tutor's responsibility to ensure this, but this should not deter students from putting forward their own suggestions and ideas for tutorial work.

4. The choice of tutorial subjects is as follows.
Students can either select four subjects from at least three of the following groups, or they can select two subjects from each of groups B and C. (In addition, they may choose an additional approved subject for one term.)
Group A: 1. The historical development of Labour Movements. 2. The development of Socialism. 3. Literature and Society, including 'Communications' and appropriate authors and texts.
Group B: 4. Social and Political Theory and Institutions, with particular emphasis on issues and institutions relevant to labour studies. 5. Labour Law. 6. Industrial Sociology, including the study of organisations (formal and informal).
Group C: 7. Industrial Economics, analysing the firm and industry, linking empirical and analytical study.
8. Management of the National Economy or Development Economics, linking national income and employment theory with current issues of planning and growth. 9. Labour Economics, linking wage theory and collective bargaining systems. Students are strongly recommended NOT to take Labour Economics until they have previously taken subjects 7 or 8.
Group D: 10. The British Trade Union Movement.
11. Comparative Industrial Relations. 12. Methods and Sources of Labour Statistics.
Schedule of Tutorial Work (a term consists of 8 tutorial weeks with written work): Terms 1, 2, 3 & 4—One tutorial subject per term, selected from the above list. (Students may opt to do half a term in Statistics, Industrial Relations, or in a previously taken subject to complete it as a major. This is most conveniently done in the 4th term. Term 5—Thesis work. Term 6—Completion of major subjects.

105

Revision tutorials for re-sits. A topic approved by tutors (programme to be agreed at the beginning of 6th term).

5. Course Requirements

Assessment and Examinations. There is a variety of methods in use in assessing a student's performance. There is a termly report on his tutorial work; there is also some form of assessment or examination on each tutorial subject. (The details of these assessments are given below.) Among the methods used are timed tests, oral examinations, and the setting of themes for written analysis. The research project is subject to oral examination. A combination of internal and external assessment is provided. In each of the subjects studied a student who reaches at least the required standard of work is graded Pass, Pass with Commendations, or Pass with Distinction.

1. The Diploma is awarded only if all course requirements are met at pass level.

2. All students taking the course will be required to attain a prescribed standard in English Expression, the elementary use of Statistics, and Industrial Relations. (a) An examination in English Expression will be set at the end of the first year. As an alternative, students may, by undertaking certain extra work, be awarded an Endorsement in this subject on their Diploma. (b) Statistics examinations will be held at the end of the 2nd, 3rd, and 4th terms, testing the work done during each of those terms. There will be, alternatively, a three-hour paper at the end of the 4th term. Students may choose either of the two methods of examination; and any student who does not reach the required standard by the first method will have to sit the three-hour examination at the end of the 4th term. (c) Examination papers, including both 'open' set themes and an unseen time test, will be set in Industrial Relations. This examination will normally be set in the final term.

3. Tutorial Subjects: Appropriate examinations will be set, normally at the end of the relevant term. Students who do not reach the required standard will be required to re-sit by the end of the 6th term.

Examination Schedule: 1st term: End of term exercise (not part of final assessment). 2nd term: 1. Examination on tutorial subject taken in 2nd term. *2. Statistics exam on 2nd term's work. 3rd term: 1. Examinations on tutorial subjects taken in 1st and 3rd terms. *2. Statistics exam on 3rd term's work. 3. Use of English. 4th term:

1. Examination on tutorial subject taken in 4th term. *2. Statistics exam on 4th term's work. *3. Statistics 3 hour paper 5th term: No examinations. 6th term: 1. Industrial Relations Examination. 2. Examination for major tutorial subjects. 3. Re-sits. 4. Thesis viva.
                    *See paragraph 5(2)(b) above.

6. Administration of the Course

The tutorial staff are responsible for the administration of the course, for ensuring that tutorial options are appropriately chosen, for deciding on grades to be awarded (with provision for external assessment) and for the general smooth running of the course. One member of staff is the Chairman of the Labour Studies Board and he is responsible to the Principal and the Vice-Principal for all Labour Studies matters.

A student who has an academic problem of any kind should normally try to resolve the matter with his current tutor. Or he may obtain assistance and advice from his advisor, or from the Chairman of the Labour Studies Board.

All students pursuing the Labour Studies Diploma, together with tutorial staff, comprise the Labour Studies Board. This meets each term, normally on a Friday afternoon, on dates which are published in advance at the beginning of each term.

The Board performs a number of functions; it discusses the progress of the course; it examines problems which may have arisen; it may discuss possible changes in the form and content of the course. Any proposed changes in regulations have to be formally approved by the Principal and Vice-Principal after consultation, if appropriate, by the Academic Board.

APPENDIX C

RUSKIN COLLEGE
TUTORIAL REPORTS AND EXAMINATION MARKS

<u>All tutors are asked to comply with the following standard
practice as agreed by the Staff Meeting</u>

1. Tutors are asked to discuss their tutorial reports with
    the student concerned before finalising them.

2. <u>Termly tutorial reports should cover the following</u>:
    a) Width of reading
    b) Depth of understanding and analytical skills
    c) Quality of written/oral expression
    d) Originality, creativity, critical judgement
        and independence of mind
    e) Is the student working to his full capacity?
    f) Likely future potential
    g) Other strong/weak points

3. Tutors are asked to give <u>tutorial assessments</u> in one of
    the following forms:
    a) An overall mark on an A - C scale, indicating the
        range of progress where appropriate, e.g. B- to B+
    b) Marks on an A - C scale on any of the heads in
        paragraph 2, especially (b) and (c)
    c) Clear and precise comments replacing marks

    A - C marks should be regarded as equivalent to

              Distinction   A
              Commendation   B++

108

Good Pass	B+
Pass	B
Weak Pass	B-
Below Standard	C

and will be so interpreted where required for College Diploma purposes.

4. Examination and test papers should be marked on the same scale.

HDH/jc 19.9.73

APPENDIX D

RUSKIN COLLEGE
APPLICATION FORM*
(SCHOLARSHIPS AND ADMISSION)

To the General Secretary, Ruskin College, Oxford

1. Name...

2. Address...

3. Date of birth..

4. Your age on leaving full-time education...............

5. Married or Single......................................

6. Dependants, if any.....................................

7. Present Occupation.....................................

8. Previous occupations (with dates):....................

9. Particulars of secondary schools attended with
dates:..

    Examination-qualifications (if any)..................

10. Give details below of any full-time courses of study
undertaken since leaving school:

---

*Editor's note: Extra spaces provided for information requested
on the Application Form are not included.

(a) Date and duration.................................

(b) Subject of course...............................

(c) Name of organising body.........................

(d) Any qualification obtained......................

11. Part-time courses undertaken since leaving school (W.E.A., Extra-mural, Correspondence, T.U. Schools, etc.)...........

Any qualifications obtained.........................

12. For which scholarship(s) do you with to be considered? (See Particulars of Scholarships and Admissions)...........

13. (a) Are you a current member of a Trade Union?........ If so, complete the following: --

Name of Union.......................................

Branch and number...................................

Length of membership................................

Any office held.....................................

Signature and stamp of Branch Secretary substantiating the above information...............................

(b) Past Membership and offices held in any trade union (with dates)..

14. Have you taken part in public affairs, local government, the co-operative movement or social work? Give particulars:
....

15. Have you held office in any other organisations? If so, give details..

16. What are your interests and activities? (Sport, cultural, hobbies, etc.):.....................................

17. How did you hear of Ruskin College? (If newspaper, state which)..

18. Why do you wish to enter the College?................

19. Which subjects or course of study interest you? (See Prospectus)..

20. Language (if any) you would wish to study (French, German, Spanish or Russian)................................

21. What would you hope to do after completing a course at Ruskin?...

22. Do you enjoy good health?..........Have you any serious disability?...
(A medical certificate will be required if you are accepted)

23. Give the names and addresses of two or three persons who may be asked for a reference, including an officer of your union, where applicable, and where possible someone who has taught you (BLOCK CAPITALS)

     (a) (Tutor)...

     (b) (Union)...

     (c) (Other)...

Successful candidates will be required to undertake to observe the regulations of the College, to devote the whole of their available time to study, and to be responsible to the Principal for their conduct during the period of their membership of the College.

I declare that the written work attached to this application is my own work.

Signature of applicant.........................Date......

APPENDIX E

WELCOMING LETTER

Ruskin College
Walton Street
Oxford OX1 2HE
August 1978

Dear Student,

We look forward to welcoming you to Ruskin for the coming year. You will be accommodated at Ruskin Hall, Headington, Oxford, a 'campus' comprising a group of accommodation blocks including The Rookery, Bowen House, Cyril Plant Building, Bowerman House, Smith House and Stoke. You are asked to arrive during the afternoon of Monday, 9 October and should report to the main building 'The Rookery' not later than 6 pm. There will be a preliminary session for all new students at 8 pm after supper. The College premises are in full use during the vacations and arrival before the day appointed for the start of a new term is not permissible, except by special arrangement (e.g. for overseas students).

The Ruskin Students Union are making special arrangements to meet incoming students on Monday, 9 October. Representative students will be in attendance at Oxford Railway Station and at Gloucester Green Bus Station from mid-morning until later afternoon on that date to meet incoming students and will arrange transport by minibus or car to Ruskin Hall.

Appendix

College fees and charges for the academic year 1978/79 have been prescribed by the Department of Education and Science as follows: Tuition fee (U.K. Students)--325 pounds; Tuition fee (overseas students) 390 pounds; Composition fee-- 20 pounds; Examination fee--20 pounds; Board/Accommodation-- 621 pounds. Where students are grant-aided by the D.E.S., or other sponsoring body and the award is for approved fees and a maintenance grant, the expression "approved fees" in- cludes tuition, composition and examination fees. The stu- dent (if resident) is responsible for the Board/Accommoda- tion charge, which should be settled promptly following the receipt of grant at the beginning of each term.

We enclose: Sketch Map; form of acknowledgment; Medi- cal Report form; Student Record form; Joining instructions; College Regulations; Notes on College Government; Notes on Domestic Arrangements.

Please read these notes carefully and let me know if there is any further information you require before arrival.

You are requested to sign the form of acknowledgment and return this to the College as soon as possible, together with the completed medical report, student record form and passport size photograph.

Yours sincerely,

C. Hopley
General Secretary

Encl.
CH/JMV

Notes

I. INTRODUCTION

1. For particulars on Ruskin graduates, see Jay Blumler, "The Effects of Long-term Residential Adult Education in Post-War Britain (with particular reference to Ruskin College, Oxford)," 2 vol. (Ph.D. thesis, Oxford University, 1962), p. 2; G. D. H. Cole and J. S. Middleton, eds., The Labour Year Book, 1919 (London: The Parliamentary Committee of the Trades Union Congress, 1919), p. 293; Stanley Pierson, Marxism and the Origins of British Socialism: The Struggle for a New Consciousness (Ithaca, N.Y.: Cornell University Press, 1973), p. 256; Paul Yorke, Education and the Working-Class: Ruskin College, 1899-1909 (Ruskin Students' Labour History Pamphlets, No. 1, April 1977), pp. 6-7; Ruskin College, Report and Accounts for Year Ended 31 July 1976 (Oxford: Ruskin College, 1976); Max Beer, A History of British Socialism, vol. 1 (London: The National Press, 1921), pp. 353-54; and G. D. H. Cole and Raymond Postgate, The Common People: 1746-1946 (London: Methuen and Co., 1938), pp. 440-71.

2. Financial distress, hostility of major unions and federations of labor, and changes in the economic, social, and political climates are among the reasons given for the disappearance of residential labor colleges. See James O. Morris, Conflict within the AFL: A Study of Craft versus Industrial Unionism, 1901-1938 (Ithaca, N.Y.: Cornell University, 1958), pp. 68-135; Lawrence Rogin and Marjorie Rachlin, Labor Education in the United States (Washington, D.C.: U.S. Department of Health, Education and Welfare, September 1968), pp. 15-20; and Ronald J. Peters and Jeanne M. McCarrick, "Roots of Public Support

for Labor Education: 1900–1945," Labor Studies Journal 1 (Fall 1976): 110–29. Illustrations of the debate on labor education, including discussions of the use of grades, exams, and other methods of student evaluation may be found in the following sources: Brian Simon, Education and the Labour Movement: 1870–1920––Studies in the History of Education (London: Lawrence and Wishart, 1974), p. 338; Geoff Brown, "Educational Values and Working Class Residential Adult Education: Some Pages from the History of Ruskin College, The Workers' Educational Association and the Labour College Movement," (n.p.: Society of Industrial Tutors, n.d.), p. 19; William W. Craik, The Central Labour College, 1909–29: A Chapter in the History of Adult Working-Class Education (London: Lawrence and Wishart, 1964), p. 14; M. Smith, "Ruskin Students 1966-8: A Study in Change," (Thesis, Ruskin College, 1974), p. 66; Henry Pelling, A History of British Trade Unionism (Baltimore, Md.: Penguin Books, 1973), p. 17; and Mil Lieberthal, "On the Academization of Labor Education," Labor Studies Journal 1 (Winter 1977): 239–41.

3. Blumler, "The Effects of Long-Term Residential Adult Education," pp. 438–39.

4. Ibid., pp. 28–29.

5. Harold Pollins, "Recent Developments at Ruskin College," The Industrial Tutor 2 (March 1977): 65–73.

6. A. W. M. Cattermole, "Residential Adult Education under Trade Union Auspices in England and Sweden: A Comparative Study of Ruskin College, Oxford, and Brunnsvik Folk High School," (Dissertation, University of Newcastle upon Tyne, 1975–76). Yorke, Education and the Working-Class. Smith, "Ruskin Students."

II. HISTORICAL BACKGROUND

1. See Yorke, Education and the Working-Class, pp. 1–3; H. B. Lees-Smith quoted the inscription on a photograph of Ruskin Hall in Labour and Learning (Oxford: Basil Blackwell, 1956), p. 50. For the life of Walter Vrooman who helped found two Ruskin colleges in the United States, see Ross E. Paulson, Radicalism and Reform, the Vrooman Family and American Social Thought, 1837–1935 (Kentucky: University

of Kentucky Press, 1968). For Ruskin's philosophy, see
Pierson, Marxism and the Origins of British Socialism,
pp. 22–38.

2. Cole and Postgate, The Common People, p. 470; Gilbert
Slater, "The Universities and the Democracy," Ruskin
Collegian 1, no. 6: 65, and G. D. H. Cole and J. S.
Middleton, eds., The Labour Year Book, 1919, p. 293. The
Vrooman quote is in Craik, Central Labour College, p. 36.

3. G. D. H. Cole, A Short History of the British Working
Class Movement: 1789–1937, vol. 3 (London: George Allen
and Unwin, 1937), pp. 51, 102, 213, and Cole and Postgate,
The Common People, pp. 470, 488.

4. Yorke, Education and the Working-Class, p. 26.

5. Anthony Giddens, The Class Structure of the Advanced
Societies (New York: Harper and Row, 1973), p. 199. Other
writers who perceive British society as characterized by a
profound sense of class differences are Everett M. Kassalow,
Trade Unions and Industrial Relations: An International
Comparison (New York: Random House, 1969), pp. 17–18;
Philip Green, "Social Democracy and Its Critics: The Case
of England," Dissent, Summer 1978, pp. 334–40; Cole and
Postgate, The Common People, pp. 470–71; and Colin Crouch,
"The Intensification of Industrial Conflict in the United
Kingdom" in Colin Crouch and Alessandro Pizzorno, eds.,
The Resurgence of Class Conflict in Western Europe since
1968, 2 vol. (New York: Holmes and Meier, 1978), vol. 1,
pp. 191–258. Richard Hoggart, The Uses of Literacy:
Changing Patterns in English Mass Culture (Boston: Beacon
Press, 1957), p. 31. Raymond Williams, Culture and Society
1780–1950 (Garden City, N.Y.: Anchor Books, 1960), p. 346.

6. Seymour Martin Lipset, The First New Nation: The United
States in Historical and Comparative Perspective (Garden
City, N.Y.: Anchor Books, 1967), pp. 246–49. For other
illustrations of class and status in Great Britain, see John
H. Goldthorpe et al., The Affluent Worker in the Class
Structure (New York: Cambridge University Press, 1973),
pp. 25–27, 177; Henry M. Pelling, America and the British
Left: From Bright to Bevan (New York: New York University
Press, 1957), p. 107; and W. G. Runciman, Relative Depriva-
tion and the Social Justice: A Study of Attitudes to Social
Inequality in Twentieth-Century England (Berkeley: University

of California Press, 1966), pp. 39-40, 50-51. Great
Britain, Department of Education and Science, Adult
Education: A Plan for Development; Report by a Committee
of Inquiry Appointed by the Secretary of State for Education and Science Under the Chairmanship of Sir Lionel
Russell, C.B.E. (London: Her Majesty's Stationery Office,
1973), p. 8 (hereafter cited as the Russell Report).

7. Craik, Central Labour College, p. 34, and Simon,
Education and the Labour Movement, p. 311.

8. Yorke, Education and the Working-Class, pp. 12-13, 19.

9. Simon, Education and the Labour Movement, pp. 319-20.
For the different attitudes of members of the working class
and of the middle class in the nineteenth and early twentieth
centuries toward adult institutes and schools established by
the middle class for workers, see Earl Hopper and Marilyn
Osborn, Adult Students: Education, Selection and Social
Control (London: Frances Pinter, 1975), pp. 39-40. Raymond
Challinor, The Origins of British Bolshevism (London: Croom
Helm, 1977), pp. 115, 161, 612. See also Geoff Brown,
"Educational Values and Working Class Residential Adult
Education," pp. 13-36. Cole and Middleton reported that
those students who organized the Plebs League did so
because they believed "that the College was drifting--
or being adroitly steered--more and more towards university
teaching and outlook, and further and further from the viewpoint of the revolutionary working-class movement," in The
Labour Year Book, 1919, p. 294.

10. See Blumler's study, "The Effects of Long-Term Resi-
dential Adult Education," pp. 368-69; Cattermole, "Resi-
dential Adult Education," p. 65; and Cole and Postgate, The
Common People, pp. 470-71. For an account of the Plebs
League by one of the principals, see Craik, Central Labour
College, pp. 29-94. For other accounts, see The Story of
Ruskin College (Oxford: Oxford University Press, 1968),
pp. 14-18; and Lees-Smith, Labour and Learning, p. 54.

11. E. J. Hobsbawn is cited in Yorke, Education and the
Working-Class, p. 26. Raymond W. Postgate, A Short History
of the British Workers (London: The Plebs League, 1962),
p. 91. See also Pelling, America and the British Left,
pp. 97, 100, 107.

12. For a more recent analysis of the split between the Plebs League and Central Labour College and the subsequent development of the latter, see Anne Phillips and Tim Putnam, "Education for Emancipation: The Movement for Independent Working Class Education, 1908-1928," Capital and Class, Spring 1980, pp. 18-42.

13. The Story of Ruskin College, p. 19.

14. For a fuller discussion of student dissatisfaction in 1967 and later and the reaction of the school, see Pollins, "Recent Developments at Ruskin College," pp. 65-69. See also, Guide Line '73, a flyer published in January 1973 by the Ruskin Students' Association in which the demands of the students are outlined.

15. Ruskin College, Report and Accounts, published annually. See also, Blumler, "The Effects of Long-Term Residential Adult Education," pp. 5, 31; David Mervin, "A View from the Present," New Epoch, 1959, pp. 13-14; and The Story of Ruskin College, p. 23.

III. RUSKIN'S ADMINISTRATIVE AND EDUCATIONAL SETTING

1. Ruskin College, Oxford Prospectus, 1978-1979, p. 4.

2. State Bursaries for Adult Education, 1978 Courses at Long-Term Residential Colleges (Stanmore, Middlesex: Department of Education and Science, 1978), pp. 1, 5.

3. Ruskin College, Report and Accounts for Year Ending 31 July 1978 (Oxford: Ruskin College, 1978), pp. 18-19.

4. Pollins, "Recent Developments at Ruskin College," p. 70.

5. Based on yearly reports appearing in Report and Accounts, 1970-79.

6. Pollins, "Recent Developments at Ruskin College," p. 67.

7. Some observations and the quotations about tutoring are based on Will G. Moore, The Tutorial System and Its Future (Oxford: Pergamon Press, 1968), pp. 19, 28-29, 32.

8. T. M. Costello, "Eliciting the Written Response," Studies in Adult Education 10 (April 1978): 28-38.

9. William H. Draper, University Extension: A Survey of Fifty Years, 1873-1923 (Cambridge, England: Cambridge University Press, 1923), pp. 78-129; K. T. Elsdon, Training for Adult Education (Department of Adult Education, University of Nottingham in association with the National Institute of Adult Education, 1975); W. E. Williams and A. E. Heath, Learn and Live: The Consumer's View of Adult Education (London: Methuen and Co., 1936), p. 108; and Robert Peers, Adult Education: A Comparative Study (London: Routledge and Kegan Paul; New York: Humanities Press, 1966).

10. Cattermole, "Residential Adult Education," p. 60.

IV.   THE RUSKIN STUDENTS

1. Blumler, "The Effects of Long-Term Residential Adult Education," pp. 383-84. Ibid., pp. 209, 211, 606.

2. Yorke, Education and the Working-Class, p. 24; Smith, "Ruskin Students," p. 3, and interview with H. D. Hughes, August 24, 1978. Some students suggested that union leaders encouraged dissidents to enter Ruskin by providing them with scholarships and references. This claim was not supported by any of the union officials or tutors I interviewed.

3. Written by a former Ruskin tutor, Lord Sanderson, in Memories of Sixty Years, quoted by Simon, Education and the Labour Movement, pp. 311-12, and by Yorke, Education and the Working-Class, p. 33.

4. Craik, Central Labour College, p. 39; Blumler, "The Effects of Long-Term Residential Adult Education," pp. 208-10, 647, and Report and Accounts, 1977 and 1978, p. 3 and p. 2 respectively. This category will receive more elaborate treatment later in this report.

5. Smith, "Ruskin Students," p. 25.

6. Figures from 1958 are from Mervin, "A View from the Present," pp. 13-14; for 1969 in Hopper and Osborn, Adult Students, p. 68, 167; also see Blumler, "The

Effects of Long-Term Residential Adult Education,"
pp. 45, 721, and Smith, "Ruskin Students," p. 5.

7. Ruskin College, Report and Accounts for the Year
Ended 31 July 1979, mimeographed (Oxford: Ruskin
College, 1979). The nonmanual or clerical occupations
continue to be the highest category of jobs formerly
held by students who enter Ruskin.

8. Blumler, "The Effects of Long-Term Residential
Adult Education," p. 381, including tables.

9. G. Brown, "Working Class Adult Education," in A. H.
Thornton and M. D. Stephens, eds., The University in Its
Region: The Extra-Mural Contribution (Nottingham: Depart-
ment of Adult Education, University of Nottingham, 1977),
p. 57; see also Ralph Ruddock, "Better Jobs for Adult
Students," Adult Education 33 (September 1960): 128.
Williams and Heath, Learn and Live, quoted by G. Brown,
"Educational Values and Working Class Residential Adult
Education," p. 4. Smith, "Ruskin Students," p. 99. See
also Blumler, "The Effects of Long-Term Residential Adult
Education," pp. 209-10.

10. Smith, "Ruskin Students," p. 96.

11. Blumler, "The Effects of Long-Term Residential Adult
Education," pp. 390, 689.

12. Yorke, Education and the Working-Class, p. 9; R. D.
Sealey, "The Social Dynamics of Residential Adult Education:
A Subjective View," in Bob Houlton, ed., Residential Adult
Education: Values, Policies and Problems.

13. Blumler, "The Effects of Long-Term Residential Adult
Education," pp. 370, 375. See also his table 18, listing
combinations of vocational, labor movement, and cultural
"stimuli" which make up 76 percent of all "stimuli" motivat-
ing his sample of former Ruskin students to enter the school,
p. 94.

14. Pollins, "Recent Developments at Ruskin College," p. 71.

15. Smith, "Ruskin Students," p. 47; Report and Accounts,
1970-78.

16. Yorke, Education and the Working-Class, p. 6, and Ruskin College, Report and Accounts, 1978, p. 2.

17. Ruskin College, Report and Accounts, 1978, p. 2.

18. Blumler, "The Effects of Long-Term Residential Adult Education," p. 318.

V. SOCIAL AND POLITICAL CLIMATE AT RUSKIN

1. For reference to Ruskin principals, see Craik, Central Labour College, pp. 35, 37-39; Yorke, Education and the Working-Class, pp. 27-35 passim; and The Story of Ruskin College, pp. 17-28.

2. Similar comments to Pollins' were made by Blumler, "The Effects of Long-Term Residential Adult Education," pp. 11-12, and Yorke, Education and the Working-Class, p. 27. Jim Hammonds, "Preparation for Social and Political Activism," in Bob Houlton, ed., Residential Adult Education, p. 64. For additional comments on the missionary role in adult education, see Graham Mee and Harold Wiltshire, Structure and Performance in Adult Education (London: Longman Group, 1978), quote is at p. 113; see also Al Nash, "The University Labor Educator: A Marginal Occupation," Industrial and Labor Relations Review 32 (October 1978): 48-49.

3. Russell Report, p. 84.

4. Siaka Stevens, "A West African Worker at Ruskin," New Epoch 1 (1943): 3.

5. The Russell Report noted that "most of the residential colleges are near to a university with which their students can associate" (p. 84).

6. Smith, "Ruskin Students," pp. 23, 88. See also Blumler, "The Effects of Long-Term Residential Adult Education," p. 147.

7. Student comment is quoted by J. H. S. Smith, "From Plough to College," mimeographed (n.p., n.d.).

8. R. Barker, Education and Politics, 1900-1951: A Study of the Labour Party (Oxford: Clarendon Press, 1972), p. 132.

9. John Lowe, <u>Adult Education in England and Wales: A</u>
<u>Critical Survey</u> (London: Michael Joseph, 1970), p. 79.

   VI. RESIDENTIAL EDUCATION AND THE PROCESS OF CHANGE

1. Russell Report, p. 85.

2. Ibid., p. 84.

3. For examples of goals of adult education, see A. A.
Liveright, <u>A Study of Adult Education in the United States</u>
(Boston: Center for the Study of Liberal Education for
Adults, 1968), pp. 3-5; Peter Stead, <u>Coleg Harlech: The</u>
<u>First Fifty Years</u> (Cardiff: University of Wales Press,
1977), p. 120; and Richard Hoggart, <u>The Uses of Literacy</u>,
pp. 71-72. Vrooman, quoted by Craik, <u>Central Labour College</u>,
p. 36.

4. Blumler, "The Effects of Long-Term Residential Adult
Education," p. 692. Pollins, "Recent Developments at
Ruskin College," p. 69.

5. For a discussion of the development of self-confidence,
see Blumler, "The Effects of Long-Term Residential Adult
Education," pp. 377 and 693; and Pollins, "Recent Developments at Ruskin College," p. 72. Quotation is from Smith,
"Ruskin College," p. 90.

6. Smith, "Ruskin College," p. 88. Pollins, "Recent
Developments at Ruskin College," p. 72. Ruskin College,
Oxford, "Evidence to the Committee on Adult Education,"
January 1970, mimeographed, appendix II, p. 2.

7. Hammonds, "Preparation for Social and Political Activism,"
p. 64.

8. Pollins, "Recent Developments at Ruskin College," p. 85.

9. Smith, "Ruskin Students," p. 75.

10. Quoted by Smith, "Ruskin Students," p. 88. Blumler,·
"The Effects of Long-Term Residential Adult Education,"
pp. 254, 302; see also "Continuity and Change among Ruskin
College Students" (report of a paper delivered to the Oxford
Sociology Society in June 1975), no author, p. 5.

Notes

11. Ruskin College, <u>Evidence to the Committee on Adult
Education</u>, p. 7. Blumler, "The Effects of Long-Term
Residential Adult Education," pp. 50-52. Smith confirmed
Blumler's finding that Ruskin graduates achieve upward
social mobility because of their additional qualifications.
Of his forty-eight respondents, 97 percent had "additional
qualifications that they sought." Only 10 percent "re-
turned to their old jobs or jobs of a similar nature."
"Ruskin Students," pp. 93-94.

12. Sir Arthur Salter, M.P., Ruskin College, <u>Activities
of Some Former Students</u> (no other information). Data are
based on Salter who explained that there were too many
Ruskin students in the local government category to
survey, so he listed eight examples of jobs in this category.

13. Ruskin College, <u>Evidence to the Committee on Adult
Education</u>, p. 8. Lord Donovan, <u>Report of the Royal Commission on Trade Unions and Employer Associations 1965-
1968</u> (London: HMSO, 1968).

14. Theodore Caplow, <u>Principles of Organization</u> (New York:
Harcourt Brace and World, 1964), p. 170.

15. Melvin M. Tumin, <u>Social Stratification: The Forms and
Functions of Inequality</u> (Englewood Cliffs, N.J.: Prentice-
Hall, 1967), pp. 18, 51, 81. Runciman, <u>Relative Deprivation</u>,
p. 40. Max Weber, "Class, Status and Power," in Reinhard
Bendix and Seymour Martin Lipset, eds., <u>Class, Status and
Power</u> (New York: The Free Press, 1966), p. 24; see also
H. H. Gerth and C. Wright Mills, eds., <u>From Max Weber:
Essays in Sociology</u> (New York: Oxford University Press,
1958), p. 241. Runciman, <u>Relative Deprivation</u>, p. 98.

16. Runciman, <u>Relative Deprivation</u>, pp. 144 ff. See also
Norman Birnbaum, <u>Toward A Critical Sociology</u> (New York:
Oxford University Press, 1971), pp. 292 ff.

17. Hopper and Osborn, <u>Adult Students</u>, pp. 110, 111, 112.

18. From a newspaper article about the student strike in
Ruskin in 1909, quoted by Craik, <u>Central Labour College</u>,
p. 76.

19. A. Burchardt, "Response to Russell: The Northern College,"
<u>Industrial Tutor</u>, March 1974, p. 2.

20. H. D. Hughes, "Looking Forward," New Epoch, 1959, pp. 15-16. Pierson, Marxism and the Origins of British Socialism, p. 256.

21. See, for instance, Ruskin College, Report and Accounts, July 31, 1977, pp. 10-11, and Report and Accounts, July 31, 1978, p. 11.

22. See also Peers, Adult Education, p. 73.

23. Russell Report, p. 85. See also Cattermole, "Residential Adult Education," p. 49.

VII. COMPARISON OF RUSKIN WITH OTHER LABOR COLLEGES

1. Russell Report, p. 44. Ruskin College, Oxford Prospectus, 1978-1979, p. 2. Information about the six residential colleges was provided by an interview with H. D. Hughes, a letter and materials from D. G. Chiles, principal of Coleg Harlech, and the following other sources: Blumler, "The Effects of Long-Term Residential Adult Education," pp. 8, 590-91, 596; Coleg Harlech, Fiftieth Annual Report, 1976-77 (Harlech, Wales: Coleg Harlech, 1977); Hillcroft College, Annual Report, 1976-77 (Surbiton, Surrey: Hillcroft College, 1976); Plater College, Annual Report 1976-77, The Catholic Workers' College (Oxford: Plater College, 1977); Newbattle Abbey College, Annual Report of the Executive Committee for 1975-76 (Midlothian, Scotland: Newbattle Abbey College, 1976); the Russell Report, pp. 45, 84; National Co-operative Education Association, Report of Education Executive, 1977 (Co-operative Union Ltd., Education Department, 1978), pp. 67-71. For recent information on Northern College, see Michael Barratt Brown, "Recent Developments in Residential Education in the United Kingdom," Labor Studies Journal 4 (Winter 1980): 237-45. For general comments on long-term residential adult colleges including Fircroft, see Bob Houlton, ed., Residential Adult Education, especially pp. 3-12. Alice H. Cook and Agnes M. Douty, Labor Education Outside the Unions (Ithaca, N.Y.: New York State School of Industrial and Labor Relations, Cornell University, June 1958), pp. 26-27, 31.

2. See Russell Report, p. 84.

125

3. Blumler, "The Effects of Long-Term Residential Adult Education," pp. 590-96, 647.

4. Cook and Douty, Labor Education Outside the Unions, pp. 77-78.

5. Ibid., pp. 78-79.

6. James W. Robinson, "The Trade Union in the Economy as a Factor in the Differential Development of Workers' Education in Great Britain and the United States" (Ph.D. dissertation, Duke University, 1967), p. 181. For further comments, see Mark Starr, "The Task and Problems of Workers' Education," in J. B. S. Hardman and Maurice F. Neufeld, eds., The House of Labor: Internal Operations of American Unions (New York: Prentice-Hall, 1951), p. 425, and Thomas R. Brooks, Toil and Trouble 2d ed., rev. (New York: Dell Publishing Co., 1971), p. 154.

7. For a discussion of the differences between "workers' education" and "labor education" and the reappearance of workers' education with some modifications under the name of "labor studies," see Richard E. Dwyer, "Workers' Education, Labor Education, and Labor Studies: An Historical Delineation," Review of Educational Research 1 (Winter 1977): 197-207.

8. James W. Robinson, "Effects of the Social and Economic Environment on Workers' Education: United States and British Examples," Adult Education Journal 19, no. 3 (1966): 172.

9. See Nash, "The University Labor Educator," pp. 43-44.

10. For an excellent survey of these schools, see Lois S. Gray, "Labor Credit and Degree Programs: A Growth Sector of Higher Education," Labor Studies Journal 1 (May 1976): 34-51.

11. For a discussion of labor colleges that once existed, see Peters and McCarrick, "Roots of Public Support for Labor Education," pp. 114-15. For a discussion of Brookwood Labor College, see Morris, Conflict within the AFL, pp. 92-97, and Thomas R. Brooks, Clint: A Biography of a Labor Intellectual, Clinton S. Golden (New York: Atheneum, 1978), pp. 65-127.

12. Quoted by Morris, Conflict within the AFL, p. 91.

13. Brookwood, Bulletin and Announcement of Courses (Katonah, N.Y.: Brookwood, 1927), p. 3.

14. Quoted by Yorke, Education and the Working-Class, p. 3.

15. Quoted by Craik, Central Labour College, p. 81.

16. "Joint Statement on Effective Cooperation between Organized Labor and Higher Education," Labor Studies Journal 1 (Winter 1977): 292.

17. Brookwood, Bulletin and Announcement of Courses, p. 3.

18. For motivations of Labor College students, see Nash, "Labor College and Its Student Body," pp. 263-65. Larry R. Matlack and Charles L. Wright, Two Nontraditional Programs of Higher Education for Union Members: An Evaluation of the Labor-Liberal Arts Program, New York State School of Industrial and Labor Relations and the DC 37 Campus of the College of New Rochelle, Industrial Research Reports, Miscellaneous Series, no. 22 (Philadelphia: Industrial Research Unit, the Wharton School, University of Pennsylvania, 1975), mimeographed, pp. 41, 43. Morris, Conflict within the AFL, p. 99.

19. Brookwood, Bulletin and Announcement of Courses, 1927, p. 13.

20. See discussion of Brookwood by Morris in Conflict within the AFL, pp. 86-110.

21. Brookwood, Bulletin and Announcement of Courses, 1927, p. 13.

22. Matlack and Wright, Two Nontraditional Programs of Higher Education, pp. 103-11 passim.

23. Empire State College, Office of Research and Evaluation, Graduates of the Labor Center, Educational, Occupational and Personal Outcomes (Saratoga, N.Y.: Empire State College, June 1978), pp. 9-11.

24. See, for instance, Sealey, "Social Dynamics of Residential Adult Education," pp. 37-40.

25. Morris, Conflict within the AFL, p. 106.

26. Cited by Morris, Conflict within the AFL, p. 92.

VIII. THE CHALLENGE TO LABOR AND ADULT EDUCATION

1. George C. Homans, The Human Group (New York: Harcourt, Brace and Co., 1950), pp. 112-13. Amitai Etzioni, A Comparative Analysis of Complex Organizations (New York: The Free Press, 1961), pp. 168-69. Etzioni also observed that liberal arts residential schools influenced the "values and character of their students." J. F. C. Harrison, Learning and Living, 1790-1960: A Study in the History of the English Adult Education Movement (London: Routledge and Kegan Paul, 1961), p. 317.

2. Cole and Postgate, The Common People, p. 470. Robert Peel is quoted by Geoff Brown, "Educational Values and Working Class Residential Adult Education," p. 53.

3. Sealey, "Social Dynamics of Residential Adult Education," p. 40.

4. See Pollins, "Recent Developments at Ruskin College," pp. 70-71, and H. D. Hughes, Ruskin College and Workers' Education--A Background Note, mimeographed handbill, February 12, 1976.

5. Ben Tillett, general secretary of the Dockers' Union, quoted in The Story of Ruskin College, p. 19.

6. Hammonds, "Preparation for Social and Political Activism," pp. 61-62. Students quoted by Smith in "Ruskin Students," pp. 95 and 66.

7. Craik, Central Labour College, pp. 61-62. For a description of the "political" approach see ibid., p. 14; Simon, Education and the Labour Movement, p. 338; Pollins, "Recent Developments at Ruskin College," p. 70; and Geoff Brown, "Educational Values and Working Class Residential Adult Education," p. 19.

8. Cattermole, "Residential Adult Education under Trade Union Auspices," p. 65.

9. For examples of the debate in the United States, see Richard E. Dwyer et al., "Labor Studies: In Quest of

Industrial Justice," Labor Studies Journal 2 (Fall 1977):
95-131; Nash, "The University Labor Educator," pp. 40-45;
and Lieberthal, "On the Academization of Labor Education,"
pp. 235-42.

10. Hopper and Osborn, Adult Students, pp. 43-49.

11. Russell Report, pp. 44 and 84.

12. Michael Barratt Brown, "Northern College," Industrial
Tutor 2 (March 1978): 3-4.

13. The H. D. Hughes quote is from Ruskin College, Report
and Accounts for Year Ending 31 July 1979, mimeographed
(Oxford: Ruskin College, 1979); see also H. D. Hughes,
"Adult Education: Russell and After," Oxford Review of
Education 3, no. 3 (1977): 283-90. Russell Report,
p. 85. See also H. D. Hughes, "Ruskin College: A Tradi-
tion of Adult Residential Education and Recent Developments,"
Industrial Tutor 3 (March 1980): 19.

14. See, for example, Hammonds, "Preparation for Social and
Political Activism," p. 62.

15. See Morris for the arguments between both sides in his
Conflict within the AFL, pp. 111-35.

16. Selig Perlman, quotes are from Hansome in "The Development of Workers' Education," p. 52.

17. Russell Report, p. 84.

Selected Bibliography

Barker, R. Education and Politics, 1900-1951: A Study of the Labour Party. Oxford: Clarendon Press, 1972.

Beer, Max. A History of British Socialism. Vol. 1. London: The National Press, 1921.

Birnbaum, Norman. Toward a Critical Sociology. New York: Oxford University Press, 1971.

Blumler, Jay. "The Effects of Long-Term Residential Adult Education in Post-War Britain (with particular reference to Ruskin College, Oxford)." 2 Vol. Ph.D. thesis, Oxford University, 1962.

Bottomore, Tom. "Structure and History." In Approaches to the Study of Social Structure. Ed. by Peter M. Blau. New York: The Free Press, 1975.

Brooks, Thomas R. Clint: A Biography of a Labor Intellectual, Clinton S. Golden. New York: Atheneum, 1978.

_____. Toil and Trouble. 2nd ed. rev'd. New York: Dell Publishing Co., 1971.

Brown, Geoff. "Educational Values and Working Class Residential Adult Education: Some Pages from the History of Ruskin College, The Workers' Educational Association and the Labour College Movement." In Residential Adult Education: Values, Policies and Problems. Ed. by Bob Houlton. N.p.: Society of Industrial Tutors, 1978.

Selected Bibliography

_____. "Working Class Adult Education." In The University in Its Region: The Extra-Mural Contribution. Ed. by A. H. Thornton and M. D. Stephens. Nottingham: Department of Adult Education, University of Nottingham, 1977.

Brown, Michael Barratt. "Recent Developments in Residential Education in the United Kingdom." Labor Studies Journal 4 (Winter 1980): 237-45.

Burchardt, A. "Response to Russell: The Northern College." Industrial Tutor, March 1974, pp. 1-2.

Caplow, Theodore. Principles of Organization. New York: Harcourt, Brace and World, 1964.

Cattermole, A. W. M. "Residential Adult Education under Trade Union Auspices in England and Sweden: A Comparative Study of Ruskin College, Oxford, and Brunnsvik Folk High School." Dissertation, University of Newcastle upon Tyne, 1975-76.

Challinor, Raymond. The Origins of British Bolshevism. London: Croom Helm, 1977.

Cole, G. D. H. A Short History of the British Working Class Movement: 1789-1937. Vol. 3. London: George Allen and Unwin, 1937.

_____, and J. S. Middleton, eds. The Labour Year Book, 1919. London: The Parliamentary Committee of the Trades Union Congress, 1919.

_____, and Raymond Postgate. The Common People: 1746-1946. London: Methuen and Co., 1938.

Cook, Alice H., and Agnes M. Douty. Labor Education Outside the Unions. Ithaca, N.Y.: New York State School of Industrial and Labor Relations, Cornell University, June 1958.

Costello, T. M. "Eliciting the Written Response." Studies in Adult Education 10 (April 1978): 28-38.

Craik, William W. The Central Labour College, 1909-29: A Chapter in the History of Adult Working-Class Education. London: Lawrence and Wishart, 1964.

Crouch, Colin. "The Intensification of Industrial Conflict in the United Kingdom." In The Resurgence of Class Conflict in Western Europe since 1968. Vol. 1. Ed. by Colin Crouch and Alessandro Pizzorno. New York: Holmes and Meier, 1978.

Draper, William H. University Extension: A Survey of Fifty Years, 1873-1923. Cambridge, England: Cambridge University Press, 1923.

Dwyer, Richard E. "Workers' Education, Labor Education, Labor Studies: An Historical Delineation." Review of Educational Research 1 (Winter 1977): 197-207.

_____, Miles E. Galvin, and Simeon Larson. "Labor Studies: In Quest of Industrial Justice." Labor Studies Journal 2 (Fall 1977): 95-131.

Eiger, Norman. "Toward a National Commitment to Workers' Education: The Rise and Fall of the Campaign to Establish a Labor Extension Service, 1942-1950." Labor Studies Journal 1 (Fall 1976): 130-50.

Elsdon, K. T. Training for Adult Education. Department of Adult Education, University of Nottingham in association with the National Institute of Adult Education, 1975.

Empire State College, Office of Research and Evaluation. Graduates of the Labor Center, Educational, Occupational and Personal Outcomes. Saratoga, N.Y.: Empire State College, June 1978.

Etzioni, Amitai. A Comparative Analysis of Complex Organizations. New York: The Free Press, 1961.

Gerth, H. H., and C. Wright Mills, eds. From Max Weber: Essays in Sociology. New York: Oxford University Press, 1958.

Giddens, Anthony. The Class Structure of the Advanced Societies. New York: Harper and Row, 1973.

Goldthorpe, John H., et al. The Affluent Worker in the Class Structure. New York: Cambridge University Press, 1973.

Selected Bibliography

Gray, Lois S. "Labor Credit and Degree Programs: A Growth Sector of Higher Education." Labor Studies Journal 1 (May 1976): 34-51.

Great Britain. Department of Education and Science. Adult Education: A Plan for Development: Report by a Committee of Inquiry Appointed by the Secretary of State for Education and Science Under the Chairmanship of Sir Lionel Russell, C.B.E. London: HMSO, 1973.

Green, Philip. "Social Democracy and Its Critics: The Case of England." Dissent, Summer 1978, pp. 334-40.

Hammonds, Jim. "Preparation for Social and Political Activism." In Residential Adult Education: Values, Policies and Problems. Ed. by Bob Houlton. N.p.: Society of Industrial Tutors, n.d.

Hansome, Marius. "Development of Workers Education." In Workers Education in the United States. Ed. by Theodore Bramfield. New York: Harper and Brothers, 1941.

Harrison, J. F. C. Learning and Living, 1790-1960: A Study in the History of the English Adult Education Movement. London: Routledge and Kegan Paul, 1961.

Hoggart, Richard. The Uses of Literacy: Changing Patterns in English Mass Culture. Boston: Beacon Press, 1957.

Homans, George C. The Human Group. New York: Harcourt, Brace and Co., 1950.

Hopper, Earl, and Marilyn Osborn. Adult Students: Education, Selection and Social Control. London: Frances Pinter, 1975.

Hughes, H. D. "Adult Education: Russell and After." Oxford Review of Education 3, no. 3 (1977): 283-90.

_____. "Looking Forward." New Epoch, 1959, pp. 15-16.

_____. "Ruskin College: A Tradition of Adult Residential Education and Recent Developments." Industrial Tutor 3 (March 1980): 19-23.

"Joint Statement on Effective Cooperation Between Organized Labor and Higher Education." Labor Studies Journal 1 (Winter 1977): 292.

Kassalow, Everett M. Trade Unions and Industrial Relations: An International Comparison. New York: Random House, 1969.

Lees-Smith, H. B. Labour and Learning. Oxford: Basil Blackwell, 1956.

Lieberthal, Mil. "On the Academization of Labor Education. Labor Studies Journal 1 (Winter 1977): 239-41.

Lipset, Seymour Martin. The First New Nation: The United States in Historical and Comparative Perspective. Garden City, N.Y.: Anchor Books, 1967.

Liveright, A. A. A Study of Adult Education in the United States. Boston: Center for the Study of Liberal Education for Adults, 1968.

Lowe, John. Adult Education in England and Wales: A Critical Survey. London: Michael Joseph, 1970.

Matlack, Larry R., and Charles R. Wright. Two Nontraditional Programs of Higher Education for Union Members: An Evaluation of the Labor-Liberal Arts Program, New York State School of Industrial and Labor Relations and the DC 37 Campus of the College of New Rochelle. Industrial Research Reports. Miscellaneous Series, no. 22. Philadelphia: Industrial Research Unit, The Wharton School, University of Pennsylvania, 1975. Mimeographed.

Mee, Graham, and Harold Wiltshire. Structure and Performance in Adult Education. London: Longman Group, 1978.

Mervin, David. "A View from the Present." New Epoch, 1959, pp. 13-14.

Moore, Will G. The Tutorial System and Its Future. Oxford: Pergamon Press, 1968.

Morris, James O. Conflict within the AFL: A Study of Craft versus Industrial Unionism, 1901-1938. Ithaca, N.Y.: Cornell University, 1958.

Nash, Al. "Labor College and Its Student Body." Labor Studies Journal 1 (Winter 1977): 253-76.

Selected Bibliography

_____. "The University Labor Educator: A Marginal Occupation."
Industrial and Labor Relations Review 32 (October 1978):
40-55.

Paulson, Ross E. Radicalism and Reform, The Vrooman Family
and American Social Thought, 1837-1935. Kentucky:
University of Kentucky Press, 1968.

Peers, Robert. Adult Education: A Comparative Study. London:
Routledge and Kegan Paul; New York: Humanities Press,
1966.

Pelling, Henry. A History of British Trade Unionism. Baltimore, Md.: Penguin Books, 1973.

_____. America and the British Left: From Bright to Bevan.
New York: New York University Press, 1957.

Peters, Ronald J., and Jeanne M. McCarrick. "Roots of Public
Support for Labor Education: 1900-1945." Labor Studies
Journal 1 (Fall 1976): 110-29.

Phillips, Anne, and Tim Putnam. "Education for Emancipation:
The Movement for Independent Working Class Education,
1908-1928." Capital and Class, Spring 1980 ("Theory
and Politics, Special Issue 10"), pp. 18-42.

Pierson, Stanley. Marxism and the Origins of British Socialism:
The Struggle for a New Consciousness. Ithaca, N.Y.:
Cornell University Press, 1973.

Pollins, Harold. "Recent Developments at Ruskin College."
Industrial Tutor 2 (March 1977): 65-73.

Postgate, Raymond W. A Short History of the British Workers.
London: The Plebs League, 1962.

Robinson, James W. "Effects of the Social and Economic
Environment on Workers' Education: United States
and British Examples." Adult Education Journal 19,
no. 3 (1966): 172-85.

_____. "The Trade Union in the Economy as a Factor in the
Differential Development of Workers' Education in Great
Britain and the United States." Ph.D. dissertation,
Duke University, 1967.

Rogin, Lawrence, and Marjorie Rachlin. Labor Education in the United States. Washington, D.C.: U.S. Department of Health, Education and Welfare, September 1968.

Ruddock, Ralph. "Better Jobs for Adult Students." Adult Education 33 (September 1960): 128-32.

Runciman, W. G. Relative Deprivation and the Social Justice: A Study of Attitudes to Social Inequality in Twentieth-Century England. Berkeley: University of California Press, 1966.

Russell Report. See Great Britain. Department of Education and Science.

Sealey, R. D. "The Social Dynamics of Residential Adult Education: A Subjective View." In Residential Adult Education: Values, Policies and Problems. Ed. by Bob Houlton. N.p.: Society of Industrial Tutors, n.d.

Simon, Brian. Education and the Labour Movement: 1870-1920-- Studies in the History of Education. London: Lawrence and Wishart, 1974.

Slater, Gilbert. "The Universities and the Democracy." Ruskin Collegian 1, no. 6: 65.

Smith, M. "Ruskin Students 1966-68: A Study in Change." Thesis, Ruskin College, 1974.

Starr, Mark. "The Task and Problems of Workers' Education." In The House of Labor: Internal Operations of American Unions. Ed. by B. S. Hardman and Maurice F. Neufeld. New York: Prentice-Hall, 1951.

Stead, Peter. Coleg Harlech: The First Fifty Years. Cardiff: University of Wales Press, 1977.

The Story of Ruskin College. 3rd ed. rev'd. Oxford: Oxford University Press, 1968.

Thornton, A. H., and M. D. Stephens. The University in Its Region: The Extra-Mural Contribution. Nottingham: Department of Adult Education, University of Nottingham, 1977.

Selected Bibliography

Tumin, Melvin M. Social Stratification: The Forms and
    Functions of Inequality. Englewood Cliffs, N.J.:
    Prentice-Hall, 1967.

Tyler, Gus. "The University and the Labor Union: Educating
    the Proletariat." Change 11, no. 1 (1979): 2-8.

Weber, Max. "Class, Status, and Power." In Class, Status
    and Power. Ed by Reinhard Bendix and Seymour Martin
    Lipset. New York: The Free Press, 1966.

Williams, Raymond. Culture and Society 1780-1950. Garden
    City, N.Y.: Anchor Books, 1960.

Williams, W. E., and A. E. Heath. Learn and Live: The
    Consumer's View of Adult Education. London: Methuen
    and Co., 1936.

Yorke, Paul. Education and the Working-Class: Ruskin
    College, 1899-1909. Ruskin Students' Labour History
    Pamphlets, no. 1, April 1977.

Acknowledgments

My thanks first go to Jozetta Srb whose skill, advice, and patience as an editor for the Publications Division, New York State School of Industrial and Labor Relations (ILR), Cornell University, were highly invaluable to me. I would also like to acknowledge the assistance provided to me by "Billy" Hughes, former principal of Ruskin College, an indefatigable educator, a gracious host, and a generous person who held Ruskin College together during the best of times and during the worst of times.

I gratefully acknowledge the contributions of two persons who each in his or her own ways, supported my interest in labor or workers' education:

Lois S. Gray, associate dean, ILR Extension, for her role in expanding the scope and depth of labor education, for increasing the academic excellence of the Extension Division, for her deep concern in reaching out to those adults who desire an education, and for her generous acceptance of those who are prone to dissent;

Robert B. McKersie, former dean of ILR, for his understanding of the role of extension in the university and for the support he provided.

I would like also to extend my thanks to Fran Benson, director of ILR Publications, for her encouragement, and to D. F. M. Horsfield, librarian, Ruskin College, who was most generous in providing assistance.

I also wish to thank Cornell University, Labor College (Empire State College), and Ruskin College for their contribution to my education.

Above all, I wish to acknowledge my respect for those adult students in the labor movement who have had the courage to return to school, and who still believe the world can be changed in our time.

Related Titles

Academic Skills: A Handbook for Working Adults Returning to School by Rebecca Thatcher

Industrial and Labor Relations Terms: A Glossary by Robert E. Doherty

Labor Relations Primer: The Story of a Union-Management Agreement by Robert E. Doherty

The Union Steward: Duties, Rights, and Status by Al Nash

Exploring the Arts: A Handbook for Trade Union Program Planners by Barbara M. Wertheimer

Apprenticeship Research: Emerging Findings and Future Trends edited by Vernon M. Briggs and Felician F. Foltman

The Miners' Fight for Democracy: Arnold Miller and the Reform of the UMW by Paul F. Clark

For descriptions of these and the many other books and pamphlets published by the New York State School of Industrial and Labor Relations, write for a free catalog of publications.

ILR Publications Division
New York State School of Industrial
    and Labor Relations
Cornell University
Ithaca, New York 14853